C000065673

My Father's Letters

My Father's Letters

Correspondence from the Soviet Gulag

The 'MEMORIAL' International Historical, Educational,
Human Rights and Charitable Society

Edited by Alena Kozlova, Nikolai Mikhailov,
Irina Ostrovskaya and Svetlana Fadeeva

Foreword by Irina Scherbakova

Afterword by Ludmila Ulitskaya

Translated from the Russian by
Georgia Thomson

GRANTA

Granta Publications, 12 Addison Avenue, London, W11 4QR
First published in Great Britain by Granta Books 2021

Original Russian edition, папины письма: Письма отцов из ГУЛАГа к детям,
first published in 2015 by the 'MEMORIAL' International Historical, Educational,
Human Rights and Charitable Society (Мемориал) of Malyj Karetny, per 12,
127051, Moscow, Russia

Published by arrangement with ELKOST Intl. Literary Agency.

The publication of this work was made possible through a grant from the
Granta Trust.

A CIP catalogue record for this book is available from the British Library

9 8 7 6 5 4 3 2 1

ISBN 978 1 78378 528 5
eISBN 978 1 78378 530 8

Typeset by Avon DataSet Ltd, Arden Court, Arden Road, Alcester,
Warwickshire B49 6HN
Printed and bound in Italy by Legoprint

www.granta.com

Contents

Foreword

By Irina Scherbakova, a founding member of the
'MEMORIAL' International Historical, Educational,
Human Rights and Charitable Society

*'This is the eighth time that I have sat down to write
to you . . .'*

This book, pieced together from the archives of Memorial, an international history and human rights organisation, tells the stories of sixteen different families through letters sent home by fathers imprisoned in Stalin's infamous Gulag system. *My Father's Letters* seeks not only to shed light on the fates of families such as these, but also to illustrate the momentous role that written correspondence has played in the preservation of family memories of repression.

Messages from prisons and camps, notes passed from neighbouring cells or thrown from trains bearing prisoners bound for a distant Gulag, and letters from relatives or loved ones to those who had been torn from their families, all constitute a significant share of Memorial's archives. This is far from coincidental. In fact, one of Memorial's primary tasks when it was founded in 1989 was to begin establishing an archive as a place of memory, both individual and collective, that would enable the recollection of the lives and fates of those who lived through this period of repression. Very often, family memories from Soviet citizens who lived through the first half of the twentieth century are limited to a couple of letters, and perhaps one or two photographs or documents, hidden in a biscuit tin or tucked away in an old briefcase up in the attic. Occasionally it was possible to save a parent's bookshelf or writing desk, but only in the event that the remaining relatives managed to avoid arrest or exile and succeeded in safeguarding the remnants of the family home. Memorial became a place where people could bring the fragments of family memories and piece them together with those of thousands of others, to form part of an elaborate jigsaw chronicling the past.

The letters donated to Memorial's archives provide a wealth of information on the lives of the men and women who sent them and they provide detailed reports of life in both prisons and camps, and in freedom and exile. Precious opportunities to relay such information had to be seized, but there was often a degree of reticence in sharing it, which was not only due to an awareness of camp censorship (if the letter was to go via official channels), but also because the fathers often wished to avoid overly distressing the recipients of their letters. The task of sharing information was far from easy, but this makes the remarkably true-to-life letters written by men such as Yevgeny Yablokov all the more important and poignant. Yablokov describes daily life in the camps in such detail that his letters read almost like a Robinson Crusoe survival story. They are testimony to man's capacity to make the most of life, and to endure.

However, regardless of how many pages were sent home, the content of some of these letters has been lost. The handwriting on notes written in black pencil under dingy barracks lighting is often bleached and illegible, and many of the scraps of paper or patches of cloth sewn together using fish bones have instead become visual evidence, artefacts and museum exhibits. Above all, the prisoner's ability or inability to communicate acquires an existential quality when considered in a historical context, for it calls to mind the well-known expression from the era of the Great Terror (1936–8): 'sentenced to ten years without the right to correspondence'. This formula was to become a euphemism for the death penalty.

Of no less importance is the insight that these letters provide into family relations among the Soviet urban intelligentsia of the 1930s and 1940s. The letters and memoirs of both senders and recipients provide a unique opportunity to assess the relationships between fathers and their children from a new angle, against the background of terror into whose revolving grindstone they had fallen.

Why is the book composed specifically of fathers' letters? Memorial's archives do, of course, contain many letters from mothers imprisoned in the Gulag. In fact, there are far more of them, due to the fact that a larger proportion of the camp survivors were women. But since many of the exchanges in this book were to be the final acts of communication between fathers and children (almost all of them were killed before they could see their loved ones again), it was decided that they would form the focus for this book. Unlike thousands of the men who perished during the Great Terror, these fathers were able to communicate, for a time at least, with those closest to them. Some were arrested in the early 1930s and shot having survived several years in prison, while others died of hunger and disease in the Gulag during the 1940s. The fathers who never returned (unlike those who did finally came home from the camps or the mothers who managed to evade arrest) were often idealised by their children, even when memories were at best vague, and often absent entirely. More often than not, those who returned from the camps, both physically and mentally broken, needed to readapt and compromise to be able to adopt a normal life again after so many years of incarceration.

All of the familial relationships explored within this book are set against the backdrop of the Soviet era, and the stories provide evidence of the horrendous pressures that families were subjected to between the 1920s and 1940s.

The Revolution had resolutely encroached on traditional family life, facilitating divorce and practically eradicating the system of inheritance and thus the ability to hand down family possessions to younger generations. During the years of the Civil War, family ties continued to weaken and disintegrate, and it was then that the authorities began to use family members as pawns. When the war ended in the 1920s, a widespread system of collective responsibility was implemented and it was announced that all members of a family were to be held responsible for the social standing of their parents before the Revolution. Children of parents labelled as 'enemies' found themselves on so-called 'disenfranchised' lists. These men and women carried with them a burden that not only deprived them of the right to vote, but also brought with it a myriad of other forms of state-imposed discrimination: they were prevented from obtaining higher education, banned from living in large cities, and often found that they were barred from employment.

However, perhaps the most terrible consequences of this system of family responsibility were experienced during the Great Terror, when the wives and children of 'enemies of the people' were subjected to repression on the direct orders of the NKVD (the People's Commissariat for Internal Affairs). Moreover, the authorities would give immunity to any wives who promptly reported that their husbands had engaged in criminal activities. Likewise, children were encouraged to denounce their parents.

How did any families succeed in countering the destructive effects of this system? This collection of letters goes some way towards providing an answer, showing the lengths that the fathers went to, to maintain communication with their wives and children and hold their families together following their arrest. This was far from easy; family relationships were often already extremely complicated, and the challenges of daily life, combined with acute housing shortages and forced separations, blurred the lines of traditional family life during the 1920s and 1930s. Maintaining ties with their children became a matter of paramount importance to the interned fathers, and one wonders whether they would have paid such close attention to the daily routines of their offspring had circumstances been different.

Astonishingly, not a single letter contains an appeal from the husband or father for his relatives to erase him from their lives for the sake of their own personal safety, despite the fact that the letters indicate that their authors were well aware that their arrests presented a constant threat to their families. Mikhail Lebedev wrote that: 'A daughter is not responsible for her father, and yet your punishment has proven to be worse than my own: soon you will not even have rations, or a roof over your head, which I at least have in prison . . .' (From a letter to his daughter, 1938).

In being deprived of all connections with their families while in the camps, the men lost their primary reasons for being. Often, their greatest fear was that they would lose their moral principles, for the support and solidarity of their loved ones at home was often the only thing that enabled them to withstand the horror. In a letter to his family in 1936, Alexei Vangenheim wrote, 'All seems gloomy, disquieting and in many ways hopeless. My home, with those dear and beloved to me, is my only source of light and joy – it is the star that lights my way.'

In order to remain close to their families, it was essential that these men maintained the attachment and respect of their wives and children. That meant dispelling doubts and convincing them of their innocence and honour. This is one of the most painful aspects of the letters, but it is absolutely key, since the questions asked by many of the children in their letters, either directly or indirectly, pertain to guilt. The dilemma was this: if the father was innocent, it follows that his imprisonment was unjust. And if this was the case, and truth was unattainable, surely the guilt lay with the State, and not the father? These questions gave rise to tortuously irreconcilable thoughts within the minds of both fathers and children, and many simply could not come to terms with their incongruent beliefs.

Almost all of the letters' authors were wholly loyal to the Soviet state, even if they were not themselves committed communists (the only author in the book to oppose the regime is Mikhail Bodrov, a Trotskyist, who despised Stalin and refused to renounce his opinions). Most remained loyal throughout their time in prison and while serving long sentences in the camps. Nevertheless, it was inevitable that their suffering in the Gulag would provoke internal battles that simply could not be resolved, despite considerable efforts to convince both themselves and their loved ones that their situation was merely a mistake that would soon be put right; that they were simply victims of a combination of tragic circumstances and false information. Some of the most tragic letters are those in which the fathers voice near-hysterical pleas to their children, imploring them not, under any circumstances, to lose faith in the Party and the Soviet regime: 'Closer to the Komsomol,* to the Party . . . Never doubt my faithfulness to the Party'; 'And remember too, that all children in Moscow, and in Lugansk and in Kharkov and in Yasnaya Polyana – everywhere, everywhere – must love Stalin, who wishes the very best to all Soviet children.'; 'And when this most dearly beloved state, the only authority acceptable to your father, demanded that he be separated from you and that he go to the deserts of Kazakhstan, your father did not curse or condemn anybody. It had to be that way, as the state required it, this state of ours that the world so needs.'

The doubt and uncertainty was hard for their children to endure, especially for the teenagers who had grown up under the influence of active and immensely powerful propaganda

---

* The All-Union Leninist Young Communist League (Komsomol) was the Communist Party's youth organisation.

systems, which had imbued them with an unshakeable faith in the Soviet regime and the Communist Party. Schools, and the Pioneers and Komsomol youth organisations, were at the forefront of the ideological brainwashing. This had a dramatic effect on the role of the family in raising children, who were instilled with a sense of mistrust towards members of the older generation and were taught that the best and most important 'educator' was the Soviet state.

Those who saw loyal fathers arrested – and were told by these same fathers that they must remain loyal to the Soviet state – were severely traumatised. Though many continued to believe steadfastly in their parents' innocence, they were nonetheless obliged to prove their loyalty to the regime, all the while living in constant fear that they might be arrested. Even decades later, the terrible consequences of conformism and irreconcilable thought were still visible: entire segments of the past were repressed in the memories of the Soviet population. It is no surprise that questions relating to the relationship between the state and the individual are so sharply reflected in the culture of those who grew up during these years of terror, and in the culture of the children whose parents were repressed, including Bulat Okudzhava, Yuri Trifonov, Vasily Aksyonov and Marlen Khutsiev,* to name but a few.

The majority of the fathers featured in this book were members of the intelligentsia; they were teachers, engineers, architects, scientists and doctors. They adhered faithfully to the principles of *Narodnichestvo*,† placing enormous value upon education, academia, professionalism and labour for the good of the people. The insistence with which they communicated their beliefs with their children demonstrates above all their understanding that

---

* Prominent Soviet cultural figures.

† A revolutionary populist movement originating in nineteenth-century Russia. The *Narodniks* were ardent believers in democracy and sought to bring enlightenment to the peasantry.

these values were their sole defence against the violence and barbarity that surrounded them. From the prisons and camps, they endeavoured to keep up with their children's education, asking about their studies, the books that they were reading and the films that they watched. They wrote poems for their little ones in the style of well-known children's writers such as Marshak and Chukovsky and created home-made books with illustrations, employing ingeniously inventive methods to ensure that their pictures would be eye-catching and colourful. For the schoolchildren, they made herbariums, drew stamps, sent postcards with reproductions of paintings from the Tretyakov Gallery, composed lists of books, offered translations and wrote notes. Even today, these letters serve as educational handbooks and unique guides to the cultural environment of the time.

Naturally, the letters often sound somewhat didactic, but they also contain numerous simple pleas for children to study hard and listen to their mothers. The fathers probably understood that their well-meant homilies might irritate their children, but these concerns were eclipsed by fears for the fates of their sons and daughters, many of whom struggled to study effectively in difficult circumstances. Would they be able to follow in their fathers' footprints, upholding family traditions by becoming engineers, doctors, architects and scientists?

Judging by their memoirs, the children interpreted their fathers' efforts to educate them as signs of how much they loved and cared for them, and as expressions of emotions that could only be conveyed through their letters. The endless worrying was entirely justifiable, for the fathers knew that their children's studies could be interrupted at any moment and that qualification in a desired profession needed to be achieved as quickly as possible. In one father's letter to his medical student daughter, written from a Kolyma labour camp, he urges her to become as well-rounded a doctor as possible, for life, he writes, could throw anything at her. The implication is clear.

The letters contain other important words of wisdom and the fathers used them to entreat their children to recognise the value of creative and useful work. For these men, languishing in labour camps, meaningful activity was of great importance and served as a counterbalance to the meaningless and back-breaking toil to which they had been condemned. The slightest opportunity to engage in any sort of significant intellectual work within the camps was a tonic to them, and consequently the letters contain numerous accounts of such activities.

Mothers play a secondary role in the letters in this book; they act as intermediaries in the dialogue between father and child. However, their lives follow a consistent pattern, with the majority of those featured doing everything within their power to keep the memory of their husbands alive, often for decades and with almost no hope of seeing them again. They raised their children alone, with only the written support of their spouses to fall back on, and even this was prone to evaporating without notice. If fate happened to spare them from the camps, women had to shoulder the burden of holding the family together in the face of the many challenges that lay ahead. Having lost their husbands, they had yet to survive the war, brave evacuation, and raise their children.

To some extent, these carefully preserved letters, reread time and again by their authors' children, corroborate lines from Vasily Grossman's novel *Life and Fate*, a novel in which letters also play a hugely important role. On the subject of the significance of the human connection in times of terror and war, Grossman writes: '. . . this very obscurity and unhappiness concealed a strange hope and clarity . . . they all knew only too well that at times like these no man can forge his own happiness and that fate alone has the power to pardon and chastise, to raise up to glory and to plunge into need, to reduce a man to labour-camp dust, nevertheless neither fate, nor history, nor the anger of the State . . . has any power to affect those who call themselves human beings. No, whatever life holds in store – hard-won glory, poverty and despair, or death in a labour camp – they will live as human beings and die as human beings, the same as those who have already perished; and in this alone lies man's eternal and bitter victory over all the grandiose and inhuman forces that ever have been or will be.'*

---

* Vasily Grossman, Life and Fate (Vintage 2006), p.846.

Translator's Note

By Georgia Thomson

This unique and poignant collection of letters is a multi-layered chronicle of love and loss, where fates intertwine and individual stories gradually snowball into a sweeping tale of systematic repression. *My Father's Letters* introduces us to just sixteen of the estimated 18 million Soviet citizens who passed through the Soviet Union's infamous Gulag system, and yet it nevertheless offers a powerful insight into the true scale and human cost of this vast network of labour camps. Indeed, so much love and emotion spills from these letters alone that it is almost impossible to comprehend the true scale of the tragedy. And yet try we must, for Joseph Stalin's sickening remark that 'If only one man dies of hunger, that is a tragedy – if millions die, that's only statistics' must never ring true. This is a book that reminds us of the human life behind every statistic and of man's frightening ability to manipulate man.

The terrible injustices suffered by these exceptionally educated and talented pillars of society also reveals a disturbing greater truth about the Gulag system: that it was a grossly inefficient economic empire where lives were pitilessly traded, at a fraction of their potential value, for economic power. Indeed, it has been said that every kilogram of gold mined in the labour camps of Kolyma cost the life of a prisoner. To put this into context, the Far North Construction Trust (Dalstroy), with which several of the men in this book served their forced labour sentences, mined 51.4 tonnes of gold in 1937 alone. By the end of the 1930s, Russia held second place in the global standings for gold output, second only to South Africa. And yet, in line with the terrible twists of fate that would come to characterise the nature of Stalin's years of repression, not even the life of the man responsible for the astonishing transformation of the Soviet gold- and oil-mining industries would be spared: Alexander Serebrovsky was shot as an 'enemy of the people' in 1938.

My motivation for translating this book came first and foremost from my admiration for the work that Memorial carries out in former Soviet states. They struggle tirelessly to highlight the importance of democracy and the rule of law, hoping that an understanding of the past will better equip people to recognise and challenge totalitarianism in future. I also feel that the book holds messages that are highly relevant today. The human mind will always be susceptible to manipulation of thought, and with the current worldwide prevalence of mass media, fake news and propaganda, we readers are in no way immune from the shadowy influence of narrow channels of information. Almost all of the fathers in this book insist upon the importance of education; they implore their children to study hard and to broaden their horizons, viewing knowledge as a tool for self-progression and a means of serving society. While most of these men astonishingly upheld their unshakeable faith in the socialist ideal until the very end, occasionally their letters reveal a flicker of uncertainty. Perhaps during these moments of doubt, some also recognised the power of knowledge as a shield against manipulation.

I would like to use this note to draw the reader's attention to instances when reading the letters when you will be placed for a moment in the shoes of the women and children receiving them, whose lives were characterised by an overwhelming sense of uncertainty. References are occasionally made to letters that we do not see, lines are erased by camp censorship and sentences cut off prematurely. I have sought to conserve these irregularities, hoping that the reader's experience of frustration and confusion on encountering them may give an infinitesimal insight into the worlds of those who had to contend with the reality of letters from loved ones that never arrived, or longed-for lines rendered illegible by the censor's pen.

I hope that you enjoy reading these wonderful letters and that they give you a sense of the extraordinary tenacity, warmth and courage of Russia's people.

Mikhail Stroikov

'I can't read my father's letters without sobbing.'

Above are the words of Yulia Volkova as she describes the letters and postcards she received from her father, Mikhail Makarovich Stroikov. Stroikov wrote to his wife, Elena, and their daughter, Yulia, affectionately known as Lyusya, from exile in Arkhangelsk, and later from the Nagaev Bay labour camp (near Berelekh) between 1935 and 1937. He was shot at a corrective labour camp in Kolyma in 1938.

Mikhail Makarovich Stroikov with his wife, Elena, and daughter, Yulia, Moscow, 1932.

Mikhail Stroikov was born in 1901 into the family of a brick-factory owner in a small village in the Kostroma region of Russia.* Stroikov attended the local parish school and is said

---

* His family were Old Believers, members of an Orthodox Christian group that had revolted against religious reforms in the second half of the seventeenth century. Their rejection of Patriarch Nikon of Moscow's liturgical reforms led to years of persecution by the authorities, until Tsar Nicholas II issued an 'Edict of Toleration' in 1905.

1

to have passed his leaving exams with flying colours, earning a certificate of merit and a copy of the Gospel for his excellent academic achievements. By all accounts, he was an extremely talented young man, and his daughter describes him as 'some sort of self-taught genius'.

Upon leaving school, Stroikov began work as a joiner in a flax mill, but his good grades soon earned him a place at the Ivanovo-Voznesensk Polytechnic Institute. In 1925, the institute put him forward to study at the Workers' Faculty of Architecture Department at Vkhutemas, Russia's State Art and Technical School in Moscow.* It came as no surprise when Stroikov was elected as leader of his university Komsomol – he had been an active member for some time and was an exemplary student, loved by both teachers and comrades alike. Indeed, the academic Vladimir Nikolaevich Obraztsov had already marked him out as a talented student and even entrusted him with the keys to his personal library.

It was during his time at Vkhutemas that Stroikov met and married Elena Alekseeva, the daughter of a musician. Their daughter, Yulia, was born in 1927, but the new father was unable to collect his wife and child from the maternity hospital – he was already locked up in Butyrka Prison. This was to be his first, but by no means his last, arrest.

Stroikov had been arrested on suspicion of an affiliation with an underground political circle and, as was so often the case, his arrest followed a tip-off by an informer. The allegations were not entirely fabricated, however, for Stroikov and his like-minded compatriots had indeed been printing and distributing leaflets criticising the politics of the Communist Party. They held it responsible for bringing about the dissolution of individual peasant smallholdings in villages and their leaflets touted slogans such as: 'They promised land to the peasants – give it back!'

---

* An art and technical institute founded by the Russian state for the education of artists and architects.

Even while incarcerated and awaiting trial, Stroikov continued to demonstrate his considerable leadership qualities by demanding improved conditions in the prison and organising a thirteen-day hunger strike in an effort to achieve his objectives. The terrible years of the Great Terror (1936–8) were yet to come, and at the time of his arrest the sentences that the authorities meted out to members of the opposition were comparatively light. Consequently, in 1929 Stroikov was sentenced to three years' exile in Kansk, Siberia. Thanks to Professor Obraztsov's intercession on his behalf, he subsequently returned to Moscow where he continued his studies at Vkhutemas. Tragically, no sooner had he returned than he was arrested once again, this time as he prepared to defend his senior thesis. His daughter was already five years old by this time and the scene of her father's arrest is etched indelibly in her memory. She said in an interview:

> It was night-time. I remember it perfectly – they shook me out of bed and when I saw them rifling through Father's writing desk – oh, how terrified I felt. How could they? It was Father's work. And how carelessly they were treating it! Well, then they seized him and took him away. And yet he still had his diploma to finish – his thesis was almost ready – all that was left to complete were the mathematical calculations. Professor Obraztsov somehow (I still do not know how) managed to persuade the head of Butyrka Prison to allow Father out into a separate isolation cell once a day, from where he was able to finish his sums. In this way, he managed to send his finalised thesis to the institute and it later emerged that his had been best of all, even without a student to defend it! Nevertheless, that student was sent to Arkhangelsk.

Stroikov spent five years in exile in Arkhangelsk where, as a now certified specialist, he worked in the city's architectural

bureau. It was from Arkhangelsk that he began his correspondence with his daughter. His letters were written on
postcards and the text was always short. He would congratulate
her on her birthday or at the start of a new school year and
sent messages wishing her health, happiness and success in her
studies. Below are a few examples:

> Sweet Lyusya,
> Today I received your letter for which I am sending you
> a big thank you. I am so happy that you will soon be
> starting school. I am sending you a big, big kiss. Your
> Papa (30.08.1935)

> Sweet Lyusya!
> In preparation for your arrival I have bought a gramophone!
> Now you will be able to dance to music. I look forward
> very much to having you to stay and am sending you a big
> kiss. Your Papa (1935)

> To my sweet daughter Lyusya,
> I am sending you a heartfelt greeting and the very best
> of wishes. Lyusya, write to me and tell me how things are
> with you and how you are getting on at school! Are
> you spending lots of time outside? Don't forget that you
> must spend some time outside in the fresh air every day
> after studying, otherwise you won't be able to study
> well. Write to me and tell me if you need me to send
> you ice skates. Sending you a big kiss. Your Papa.
> (24.10.1936)

> Sweet Lyusya!
> Thank you very much for your letter. I am so happy that
> you enjoyed the books by Pushkin and that your lessons
> at school are going so well. I am only sorry that I could

not watch you dance the Polonaise. I hope to see this soon though. I am sending you a big kiss. Your Papa. (07.02.1937)

Stroikov's interest in his daughter's cultural upbringing was not limited to her reading material. He also wrote her carefully chosen postcards featuring printed reproductions of paintings found in the Tretyakov Gallery. In an interview she said:

> Papa specifically bought postcards printed with paintings from the Tretyakov Gallery so that I would become acquainted with art. At one point he had dreamed of becoming an artist himself. He bought me all of the postcards from the Tretyakov Gallery and also books by well-respected authors, building up a library for me. And when I went to visit him, I had my own shelf, which was lined with rows of books. They were explicitly for me – suited to my age – and concerning every topic imaginable. I really loved Cosette* – I remember crying my eyes out over her. I also adored 'The Black Book' and 'Schwambrania' by Lev Kassil and 'Tales of Wild Animals for Children'. Father assembled a wonderful library for me. There were many books that I kept, including, of course, Pushkin. Naturally, all of Pushkin's fairy tales featured on the bookshelf – these were considered compulsory reading. On 21 November, my birthday, I would receive a parcel from him – it always contained a new book of some description. To this day, I adore books, and perhaps I have my father to thank for this.

While in exile, Stroikov was appointed head architect at the building group Arkhbumstroy, the enterprise responsible for the

---

* Cosette: a character in Victor Hugo's novel *Les Misérables*.

Father's Corner

construction of the Arkhangelsk pulp and paper mill, which still operates today. This enabled him to move into a small room, or rather a screened-off corner of a room, which he rented from a landlady. He wrote:

> Lyusenka, I now have a steady job. You can come and
> visit me.

His wife and daughter travelled to Arkhangelsk to see him, but they were not allowed to live together as a family – his wife was forbidden from staying in the same house. Nevertheless, Stroikov managed to obtain permission for his daughter, who by this time had finished her first year at school, to stay with him for a little while.

In an interview Yulia said:

> I remember the first time that I went to stay with Papa, he told me to go outside into the courtyard to meet the other children and make friends. At first they hit me because I was from Moscow, and I ran to complain to my father. He said, 'Don't you dare come complaining to me. You must either reach an agreement or fight back. That way they will come to respect you.'

Father and daughter lived together from the summer of 1936

until January 1937. The NKVD refused to allow Stroikov to extend their time together and, according to his daughter, this struck a warning note for him. His sense of foreboding increased further when his official business trip to Moscow fell through following the NKVD's refusal to hand over his passport. Another arrest followed soon after.

His landlady in Arkhangelsk remembers his third arrest. Secret police officers had reportedly arrived at the house saying, 'Mikhail Makarovich, bring your drawing instruments, paper and books with you – they will all come in useful.' She had heard him answer, 'Nothing will be of use to me any longer.'

Nevertheless, reassuring and optimistic letters continued to arrive with his family in Moscow from various legs of his prisoner transport – from Sverdlovsk,* Vladivostok and Nagaev Bay. Stroikov still hoped that he would simply be resettled in exile and that he would be able to take his family with him for, after all, there could surely be no new accusations on which to base a sentence.

Stroikov wrote to his wife on 14 July 1937:

> Sweet Lena,
> Today I received the verdict on my case from the
> Special Board of NKVD and as a result I also have the
> opportunity to update you on a few things at my end.
> But I don't know where to direct my letters – are you in
> Moscow now, or in Ark-sk . . .? So I'm writing to both
> addresses.
>   First of all, for my part I'm trying hard to obtain
> permission for us to meet soon. As I send this letter I am
> also giving a statement to the northern regional NKVD,
> requesting that they allow me a meeting with you and
> Lyusya.

---

* Today Yekaterinburg.

Secondly, if you are here, please package and send me the following things: an autumn coat in exchange for my winter one, brown trousers and big jumper, 2 sets of underwear, a towel, handkerchiefs, socks, a penknife, a razor and mirror, bedclothes, a duffel bag and a small suitcase. That's it, thank you. As for the other things, do with them as you see fit. I cannot ask you for money as I don't know whether you even have any yourselves. I hope to receive payment for my work while I am on the train – I'm not sure how much they will give me for the holiday time that I have not taken.

They gave me 5 years in a north-eastern labour camp (Far East), but for what, I myself do not even know, since no charges have been filed against me. It must be something from 1927–28.

Don't worry and don't lose hope. Stay healthy for Lyusya. I will petition for a pardon. I hope this letter finds you and that we will see each other soon. I cannot say when they will release me, but it looks like it won't be long . . . perhaps in 5 or 6 days. Try to reply to this letter straight away so that I know where you are and to where I should direct my letters. Write to me at this address: Arkh[angelsk], Proletkult Street, 14. Arkh-prison No. 1, and address it to me.

I am sending you both a big kiss and wish you both good health. I myself am well.

Your Misha (14.07.37)

Stroikov sent letters but was mystified when he received no reply. Sadly, it transpired that his wife and child had not received them – an acquaintance in the NKVD had advised Elena to leave Moscow and, heeding his warning, she and her daughter had moved to Pushkino, a city about thirty kilometres from the capital. Unaware of this development, Stroikov continued to direct his letters to the family's Moscow address. Meanwhile, Elena and Yulia had been writing to him in Arkhangelsk, but the NKVD had forbidden his former landlady from informing them that he had been transported to Kolyma. Extracts of letters from Mikhail Stroikov to his wife show his anxiety:

> Sweet Lena! I have already sent you several letters – I don't know whether you received them? [. . .] It's just that I'm stumped – 5 months have already passed with no news from you, and this truly alarms me. (18.07.37)

> Sweet Lena! If you received my letters from Arkhangelsk and Vologda then you will know that I have been condemned by the Special Board of NKVD under Article 58-10 to 5 years and am heading to a corrective labour camp in the Far East. The fact that I have heard absolutely no news from you for the last 5 months really worries me. I do not know where you are, in what conditions you are living, whether you and Lyusya are well . . .(05.08.1937)

Mikhail Makarovich Stroikov was shot on 13 August 1938 in the Sevvostlag, not far from the small village of Berelekh in the Magadan region. His wife was told that he had died from meningitis.

In an interview his daughter Yulia said:

> I will never forget how my mother and I went round to our friends and took out the map to find Berelekh station [. . .] I never thought he was guilty. I adored my father and believed wholly in his integrity, his exceptional integrity. He said exactly what he thought. He was never false. I waited for him to return, waited from noon until night. I believed that he was still alive. I can't read my father's letters without sobbing.

A letter from M.M. Stroikov sent from Sverdlovsk (now Yekaterinburg) during his prisoner transport to Koymya, 05.08.1937.

Mikhail Makarovich Stroikov's daughter lived up to his expectations, graduating from the Moscow Higher College of Arts and Industry (the former Stroganov Institute) and becoming a stage and set designer in several of Moscow's theatres.

Alexei Vangenheim

'Pass on my enthusiasm to her'

Alexei Vangenheim wrote his letters home to Moscow from the Solovki labour camp (on the Solovetsky Islands), where he had been sent following his arrest in January 1934. He remained there until 1937, when he was shot upon the orders of a Troika of NKVD. His letters were addressed to his wife and young daughter, Eleonora, who was only three years old at the time of his arrest. Alexei's wife, Varvara

Alexei Feodosevich Vangenheim, 1910.

Kurguzova, was headmistress at School Number 40, described at the time as an establishment for 'late starters'.*

Vangenheim penned a remarkable total of 168 letters from Solovki, of which 141 still survive today, thanks to the efforts of his wife and daughter. These letters allow us a glimpse into the thoughts, fears and hopes of a highly intelligent and remarkable man.†

---

* Children who, for various reasons, began their schooling late. Some did not commence primary school until the age of twelve or thirteen.

† Fragments of his letters also appear in the book *Alexei Feodosevich Vangenheim* by V. V. Potapov and E. A. Vangenheim.

> *'I voluntarily rejected all the advantages of the social
> class into which I was born.'* (An extract from a letter
> written 20 February 1934)

Alexei Vangenheim's life could have taken him down an altogether different path. He was born into a family of landowners in 1881 – a report written by the Troika of NKVD condemning him to death (dated 9 October 1937) describes him as 'the son of a nobleman and major landowner'. His father, Feodosi Vangenheim, had been a father of eight, a village intellectual and a member of the local land council, who managed to construct a meteorological observation station and testing field on his farmstead. The origins of the family name are disputed, but it is likely that they had Dutch or German ancestry.

Alexei was the second eldest son, and his education got off to a good start at home, where he learned to read and speak in both German and French. He attended the local grammar school – Oryol Gymnasium – before moving to Moscow to study at Moscow State University and the Moscow Agricultural Institute.

During the First World War, Vangenheim was appointed manager of the Eighth Army Weather Service and later, on the south-western front, he was promoted to the rank of colonel. His role in the organisation of a gas attack on the Austrian army earned him a ceremonial golden weapon. He was in such a position of favour that had he wished to follow the example of his brother Nikolai[*] and emigrate to France after October 1917, he could easily have done so. Instead, he inadvertently chose a very different fate.

---

[*] Nikolai Feodosevich Vangenheim (1880–1967). A member of the White movement (a loose confederation of anti-Bolshevik forces that fought against the Red Army during the Russian Civil War of 1917–22), he served in Markov's Volunteer Army. He emigrated to France from Kharkov in 1919 and worked as a military engineer. Died in Chelles. Information about him appears in *Unforgotten Graves: Russian Abroad: Obituaries in Six Volumes, 1917–1997* (Moscow, 1999).

By the time he took up his studies at the Faculty of Physics and Mathematics in Moscow, Vangenheim was already a devotee of socialism, and as such he was an active participant in student unrest. After the October Revolution, he became involved in organising the 'revolutionary education' of the population of Dmitriyev, directing the education and activism of the peasant farmers of Kursk Province.

In June 1919 Vangenheim founded the museum in Dmitriyev that is now named after him. In July 1921, he was appointed the district's chief agronomist and took part in the launch of a weather bureau in Kursk Province. Far from being just an amateur hobbyist, the dedicated young scientist elected to continue his studies at the Moscow Agricultural Institute while working for the Snug weather bureau, which had been named by his father.

It was in the 1920s that meteorology became the most important part of young Vangenheim's life. Having arrived in Petrograd* in 1923, he began work as a weather forecaster in the Department of Long-Range Weather Forecasting in the Central Physics Observatory (CPO), under the direction of the future academic and famous meteorologist Professor Boris Multanovsky. By 1925 he was a member of the CPO's management team and contributing to the publication of two journals: *Climate and Weather* and the *Geophysics and Meteorology Journal*. He also delivered lectures at sessions of the Russian Geographical Society's Meteorological Committee.

Vangenheim returned to Moscow in 1926 to take up the post of deputy director of the Science Institute of the Central People's Commissariat for Education for the RSFSR (Russian Soviet Federative Socialist Republic). Two years later he was appointed a professor at Moscow University, officially joined the Bolshevik Party (though he had been a member of the Russian

---

* Today St Petersburg.

Social Democratic Labour Party even before the Revolution), and became a general committee member for the State Council of Science. He had a pass enabling him to come and go freely from the Kremlin and associated with the likes of Anatoly Lunacharsky,* Lenin's wife Nadezhda Krupskaya, and various people's commissars. Both Maxim Gorky and Otto Schmidt† visited his apartment, along with numerous foreign scientists on visits to the USSR. And when, on 28 August 1929, members of government voted to implement one of his initiatives – creating a united hydro-meteorological service (the Hydro-Meteorological Committee of the USSR) – Alexei Vangenheim was nominated as its president.

Alexei Vangenheim with his
daughter, Eleonora, Moscow, 1931.

In time, he settled into family life, marrying Varvara Kurguzova, whom he had met in Dmitriyev several years earlier. A much-adored daughter, Eleonora, was born shortly afterwards

---

* A Russian Marxist revolutionary and Soviet politician, writer and critic. Anatoly Lunacharsky was an active participant in the 1917 October Revolution and became the first People's Commissar for Education.

† A Soviet scientist, astronomer, geo-physicist and mathematician, Schmidt was a member of the Communist Party and awarded the title 'Hero of the Soviet Union', the highest distinction in the Soviet Union, in 1937.

and her father nicknamed her '*Zvezdochka*'.* The future seemed bright and the former nobleman believed that he finally had it all: his work, his family and his country.

Vangenheim was arrested on 8 January 1934. He and his wife had tickets to go to the opera that evening, but Varvara waited in vain on the steps of the Bolshoi Theatre for her husband to arrive.

Following a short investigation into the standard accusations of spying and sabotage, his sentence was announced: ten years in a corrective labour camp.

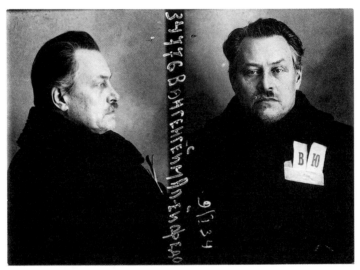

Prison photograph, 1934.

In his letters from the Solovki camp, Vangenheim often remembered his efforts to educate the peasants in Dmitriyev, as well as his later work as president of the USSR's Hydro-Meteorological Committee. On 24 August 1935 he wrote: 'In spite of everything, I have no doubt that my prediction regarding the unification of the global meteorological services will prove correct.' These memories were painful. Pride in his achievements was closely intertwined with extreme hurt and resentment.

---

* Translator's note: A nickname comparable to 'Little Star'.

An alarm rings involuntarily in my soul, warning that the
truth is redundant. (14.07.1934)

When I remember . . . my work at the Hydro-
Meteorological Committee and my brainchild, the
Hydro-Meteorological Service, which I nurtured and
cherished out of pride for the USSR, my thoughts take
on a terrible, painful quality that makes me want to
scream out loud. (09.11.1934)

I remember the many tens of lectures I gave in towns
and villages between 1918 and 1922; at that time I never
undertook a single journey without giving a lecture of
some sort. At first, I would talk about the fundamentals of
socialism and the tasks facing the Soviet leaders, often using
homemade projection slides to accompany my lectures. I
brought the idea of the dictatorship of the proletariat and the
uncompromising war on religion to the peasants with such
firm belief in my mission. How many agricultural lectures
I gave and organised for people across all those districts, not
to mention for the youths on the pre-conscription military
training programmes! All of this is now of course forgotten,
since somebody considered it necessary to slander me in this
absolutely absurd manner. (17.04.1936)

Despite the pain, he continued to revisit his memories. In a
letter to his wife he mused:

Time will pass, and everything will be forgotten. All that
I accomplished in my working life will be forgotten. And
so I have decided to summarise a little of what I achieved,
so that you and my daughter may know that I did not idle
my life away in vain.

Vangenheim had evidently already lost all hope of seeing his family again. He hurried to recollect and express all that he had managed to achieve, and all that which he had hoped to accomplish but had been unable to realise.

> In a recent journal I read an article about the use of wind
> power in the construction of a socialist state [. . .] This
> energy, if used judiciously, could provide us with tens
> of thousands of Dneprostrois (Dnieper Hydroelectric
> Station) and would enable us to fight drought, especially
> in deserts where heat and winds are at their most extreme
> and to where it is exceptionally difficult to deliver fuel
> for machinery. Wind could turn these deserts into oases.
> The prospects are dazzling, even before we consider
> that in the north, the wind is not only able to provide
> energy for heating and lighting, but also for cooking and
> transportation. [. . .] I recall that I was the first person not
> only to raise this idea, but also to set it in motion, having
> included the 'Wind Cadastre' into the plan [. . .] By 1934
> I was due to have completed the first atlas of wind energy
> distribution patterns in the USSR. Of course, it will still
> be published, just without me. The same goes for the
> so-called 'Solar Cadastre', also my brainchild, designed to
> record solar energy in the USSR. [. . .] The future rests
> on solar and wind energy, since it is inexhaustible and
> colossal in the scope of its power, and yet it seems to me
> that my departure will suspend any opportunity to make
> use of it for several years to come. (10.06.1935)

> Questions relating to the troubles of mankind, of
> releasing labour from the yoke of weather, perhaps also
> on the prolongation of life . . . are of great interest to
> me. Therefore, in early 1932, I called together the first
> conference in the Soviet Union, and I think perhaps

even the first conference in the world, on the impact of weather and the hydrological system on mankind. Articles reporting on this All-Soviet conference were featured in 'Pravda', 'Izvestiya' and my own journals. It proved to be an extremely interesting meeting, attended by our experts, doctors, architects, engineers, policymakers and forestry specialists. Questions were raised on 3 fundamental problems: 1) The hydrological system and people's health from a medical perspective. 2) The hydrological system and the construction of buildings. 3) The hydrological system and city planning and landscaping. There was enormous interest. I felt like the man of the moment. The conference resulted in the creation of a commission, with myself at its head. [. . .] Incidentally, a task was set to study the condition of man in a variety of climatic settings: in the Arctic; in high–altitude mountains; in the middle of the plains; in the desert. Plans relating to Spitsbergen, where I was overseeing a special station, were drawn up with the aim of attracting distinguished doctors. [. . .] My conference received recognition and responses from abroad. The Pasteur Institute invited me to attend a similar meeting to be conducted in Paris based on our own example. (30.06.1935)

The USSR possesses an enormous wealth of hydroelectric power, or white coal, as we call it. If we take all of the water in our vast territory into account, we are capable of building tens of thousands of Dneprostrois, Volkhovskayas (a hydroelectric plant on the Volkhov River) etc. [. . .] In 1931, I came up with the idea of organising a water cadastral survey for a socialist country, but before the planning stage could get underway, we needed to obtain accounting records. I spent a long time at the Gosplan (State Planning Committee) and at the People's Commissariat for Finance in order to obtain the necessary financial resources but in the end I received nothing but casual sympathy. [. . .] There were further trials to endure, including the self-serving greed of the specialists, a shortage of people to work on the project, a deficit of experience, and the failure by several institutions to disclose data. All of these factors hindered the progress of the project. Nevertheless, by the time the 15th Congress took place, the Party had managed to get the cadastral survey onto a stable track and had guaranteed its completion. I do not know the current status of this matter. (24.06.1936)

Vangenheim was clearly extremely influential as a driving force behind the organisation of the Soviet Union's hydro-meteorological services. Having created a united meteorological system in the USSR, he dreamed of uniting the weather services of the entire world. In his quest to achieve this goal he created the Main Geophysical Observatory and the State Hydrological Institute. He also edited the journal *The Herald of the United Hydrological Services of the USSR*, and both organised and gave lectures at the Hydrological Conference of Baltic Countries in Leningrad. Furthermore, he sought the assistance of Tor Bergeron, an eminent Swedish scientist who was a founding father of studies on air masses and weather fronts. It was on Vangenheim's initiative too that the first specialised educational institutions in the world – the Moscow and Kharkov hydro-meteorological institutes – were founded (alongside several technical training schools), which incorporated studies of the north into the national teaching programme of the USSR. In keeping with his passion for long-term weather forecasting, Vangenheim constructed an entire network of weather stations across the Soviet north.

The network was vast and the weather stations were built in the furthest backwaters. It was not without its mistakes, of course, but we did the very best we could. The series became the pride of the Soviet Union. Bergeron praised it very highly. (24.07.1935)

I am sure you are reading about Levanevsky's forthcoming flight* over the North Pole. Strange as it may seem, this is a matter that concerns me very, very closely. I reluctantly recall all that I did for him, for if I had not struggled for three years to install the network of polar stations, his flight would have been impossible. (03.08.1935)

Vangenheim was just fifty-two years old when he was arrested and torn away from his beloved projects. With his ambitious plans, the scope of his physical and creative powers and his boundless devotion to socialism, one cannot help reflecting on how much more he could have achieved.

He was arrested on 8 January 1934. What were the grounds for his arrest? This question was to become superfluous during the years of the Great Terror (1937–8), but these years were still some way off and his foreign surname and non-proletarian background should not have constituted sufficient cause for condemnation in 1934. After all, he had never engaged in Trotskyism, nor was he a member of any type of opposition group. The murder of Sergei Kirov,† which marked the

---

* Sigizmund Levanevsky was a Soviet pilot and pioneer of long-range polar flights. On 3 August 1935 he attempted a transpolar flight from Moscow to San Francisco in a single-engine long-range bomber. He was forced to abort the mission one thousand miles into the flight, when the oil tank began to leak. A Hero of the Soviet Union, he died in 1937 during another attempt to pilot a bomber across the North Pole from Moscow to Alaska.
† Sergei Kirov was a prominent Soviet politician and close friend of Joseph Stalin. His assassination in 1934 was used as a pretext to launch a mass wave of repression.

beginning of widespread mass repression, was still one year away. So the question remains, why?

Yuri Chirkov, a future doctor of Geographical Sciences serving time in the Solovki labour camp alongside Vangenheim (Chirkov had been arrested at the age of just fifteen), spent a lot of time talking to and getting acquainted with his comrade. He recalls Vangenheim's own thoughts on the reasons behind his arrest:

> In 1933 the first All-Union Geophysical conference took place in Leningrad, attended by foreign scientists from many different countries. On the invitation cards it was stated that Alexei Vangenheim's opening address would be given in French. Approximately an hour before the conference was scheduled to begin, Vangenheim received a telephone call from Stalin, who instructed him to deliver the speech in Russian. A surprised Alexei Vangenheim explained that the programme had already been agreed with all the relevant authorities, and that to make changes to it at this stage would be impossible, as the schedule had already been published. The speech went ahead in French, yet despite the dazzling success of the conference, Vangenheim sensed that attitudes towards him had shifted. A few months later, in January 1934, the Osoaviakhim-1 high-altitude balloon crashed on descent from its record-breaking maiden voyage, killing all three crew members on board, and Vangenheim was accused of deliberately predicting the conditions of the flight erroneously.

Chirkov's version of the story explains very little. The speech given in French, contrary to instructions, was hardly a very serious matter, although Stalin was not in the habit of forgetting such 'disobediences'. Moreover, the Osoaviakhim-1 high-altitude balloon disaster occurred on 30 January 1934,

22   MY FATHER'S LETTERS

two weeks after his arrest, and could only have been used to condemn him if the dates of his arrest were tampered with. We can only assume that by the time he was arrested, Vangenheim had been under the close observation of the OGPU* for some time. As likely as not, he had probably been 'under suspicion' from as early as 1931, when he took up the post of deputy chairman of the Central Bureau of Regional Local History.

The reality of the matter was that the press, at the behest of the Kremlin, had begun to hound local history specialists in the early 1930s for their efforts to safeguard relics of the past and preserve important natural landmarks. Vangenheim, the future editor-in-chief of the journal *News from the Central Bureau of Soviet Local History* and later also the *Soviet Local History* journal, took the old 'bourgeois' historians under his protection as far as he was able. As a result, he was ousted from his position as editor-in-chief of *News from the Central Bureau of Local History Specialists* in 1931, and shortly afterwards he was also relieved of both his place on the editorial board of the same journal, and the panel of the Central Bureau of Local History Specialists. Later that year, an article in *Soviet Local History* accused Vangenheim and his colleagues of displaying 'a liberal attitude' towards the study of old local history.

As for the Osoaviakhim-1 balloon disaster, despite the government commission's conclusion that the meteorologists were blameless, for the secret police the disaster could not have occurred at a more opportune time. Vangenheim was arrested, with several of his colleagues, and charged with organising counter-revolutionary activities within the Soviet Hydro-Meteorological Service and enlisting the help of his co-workers to achieve his goal.† He was alleged to have carried

---

* OGPU or Joint State Political Directorate was the name given to the secret police for the Soviet Union between 1923 and 1934.
† There appear to be some inconsistencies around the date and pretext for Vangenheim's arrest. It is possible that the date of his arrest was misrecorded,

out intelligence work, gleaning secret tip-offs from among the specialists working in the weather service, and was accused of sabotage; namely giving false weather forecasts with the aim of bringing about the failure of the agricultural campaign. The criminal case report states that, 'He did not confess personally to the charges, but was incriminated by the testimonies of Kramaley, Loris-Melikov and Vasiliyev.' In 1956, during the long process of rehabilitation, both Loris-Melikov and Vasiliyev retracted their statements, admitting that they had incriminated both themselves and Vangenheim 'as a result of the use of unlawful interrogation methods and practices by the authorities'.

During the years he spent at Solovki, Alexei Vangenheim never abandoned his belief that he had been dealt an injustice. He wrote to Stalin, Mikhail Kalinin, Lazar Kaganovich, Nikolai Yezhov, Andrei Vyshinsky, Georgi Dimitrov, the Party Control Commission (he sent them eight letters in total), and also to his wife, whom he asked to find out what had become of his petitions. He asked her to appeal to his eminent friends (Maxim Gorky, Nadezhda Krupskaya, Otto Schmidt and others) for help.

> I would ask you to go to Tikhon Alexandrovich Yurkin*
> (at the government building in the Zamoskvorechny
> District) as soon as you have a minute, and to find out
> whether he received my letter and has done anything
> about it. I ask only that he and Comrade Stalin hear
> me out. This is all that is required for truth to prevail.
> (23.05.1934)

---

but seems more likely that he was arrested and only charged some weeks later when, conveniently for the secret police, the Osoaviakhim balloon crashed on its maiden voyage.

* Tikhon Alexandrovich Yurkin (1898–1986). In 1934 he was People's Commissar of state-owned farms growing crops or raising livestock in the USSR.

Find out whether or not Comrade Stalin received my
formal letter from 11 May . . . I simply cannot believe
that it will go ignored. I have one other errand for you
– go to the Party Control Commission of the All-Union
Communist Party (Bolsheviks) and find out whether they
received my appeal claim, and what the result is . . .

You cannot imagine how a person feels when he has
fulfilled all of his sacred communist duties and yet is
unable to achieve any real results. There is hurt, pain,
and an awareness of a wild and maddening powerlessness.
But I have not yet lost faith. I wrote to Comrade Stalin
on 9 March, affirming that my belief in the party and the
Soviet Central Committee has not been shaken and that
under no circumstances will I lose faith in either. Of this I
am certain.

There are moments when my faith wavers, but I fight
these feelings systematically and will not let them get the
better of me. A. M.* once sang about the pride and tragic
beauty of man. Why can't he physically demonstrate that
he can fight for the honour of a Communist who remains
a proud Leninist to this day? (05.06.1934)

I sent an official petition to Comrade M. I. Kalinin on 6
June [. . .] Somehow I cannot believe that my request is a
mere voice crying out in the desert. I will wait. I have not
yet lost hope. (18.06.1934)

Hope faded with every passing day. His letters to party officials
went unanswered, and efforts made by his wife to enlist the help
of former family friends came to nothing. Vangenheim idealised
the Communist Party and Soviet state as before, but his faith in
its leadership was in tatters.

---

* A. M. Gorky.

Still nothing has come of my address to Comrade Stalin on 11.05.34, nor has there been word following my letters to the P[arty] Control C[ommisson] and TSIK [Central Executive Committee] on 17.05, or from Comrade Kalinin, whom I petitioned on 6 June. I do not know what to think. Somehow I do not wish to consider the possibility that nobody is interested in the real truth. I respect the Party and Soviet powers sufficiently so as to not lose hope that their representatives will be interested in hearing the truth. (07.07.1934)

My appeals to Comrades Stalin, Kaganovich and Kalinin, and the statement that I sent to the visiting commission have so far yielded no results. An alarm rings involuntarily in my soul, warning that the truth is redundant. Terrible doubts are creeping up on me against my volition. For the moment I am managing to chase them away. (1934)

Did you go to A. M.? Everybody here speaks ill of him – they remember his visit well.* (14.07.1934)

Could you possibly find out from O. Y.† whether he received my appeal to Comrade Stalin dated 11.05.34. A long time has passed. Surely it cannot be that not one of my letters has reached its destination? (23.07.1934)

---

* Maxim (Alexei Maximovich) Gorky visited Solovki in the spring of 1929. In spite of the hopes of Vangenheim's fellow prisoners who believed it would be impossible to 'pull the wool over Gorky's eyes', the writer did nothing to alter the course of their fates for the better. Moreover, he did not even attempt to do so, wholeheartedly believing the lies fed to him by the members of the secret police escorting him around the camp. Information regarding Gorky's time at Solovki can be found in *Reflections on the Russian Soul: A Memoir* written by Dmitry Likhachov who was a prisoner on the island in 1929.
† Here he refers to Otto Schmidt. According to Alexei Vangenheim's wife, she was unable to obtain an answer to this question from Schmidt – he simply refused to open the door to her.

> Intuition tells me that this suffering is unlikely to end
> soon. All that has happened and all that surrounds me
> contribute to an ever-mounting sense of pessimism. I
> want to fight it, and indeed I do fight it persistently, but
> every day, as if by design, the facts rise up and seek to
> reinforce my pessimism. (13.01.1935)

The year following Vangenheim's arrest had been filled with futile hopes, but ultimately it ended just as expected; in despair. For many of those who shared his fate, the initial sense of disappointment at circumstances that remained unchanged was succeeded by a reorientation in world views, a revolution in thought and a rejection of former ideals. Such was the case for many victims of Soviet-era repression, but not for Alexei Vangenheim.

'Even at Solovki it is possible to build socialism.'
(From a letter dated 11 May 1934.)

Vangenheim was initially assigned to the camp's agricultural labour detail. He worked in the greenhouse vegetable garden and described in one of his earliest letters home, '10-hour working days from 6 a.m. until 4 p.m. without breaks or rest'. Nevertheless, despite the punishing regime, he voluntarily took up his customary educational work among his fellow prisoners: 'I work by day, and in the evenings, I give lectures . . .' (20.05.1934) Among the topics he covered in his lectures were exploration of the stratosphere, reaction engines, conquering the Arctic, flights to the Moon, the use of solar energy, the Northern Lights, solar eclipses, the application of science in the everyday, radiation energy, solar physics and the possibility of life on Mars.

He wrote with pride about his efforts to educate his fellow prisoners:

In some instances, especially when my audience is composed primarily of criminals, my lectures are received attentively and people absorb the information hungrily. For me, this is an exercise in the popularisation of Science. I tailor the majority of my lectures towards the less-educated listener and I seek to enunciate ideas that are sometimes very complicated in layman's terms. The only reason that I do not tire of giving these lectures is that they do bring me a certain amount of pleasure, albeit it to a nominal degree. (18.04.1936)

I am now a specialist in giving lectures to people who do not wish to listen to them. This was certainly the case the first time I was invited into one particular cell that I took under my wing. However, as soon as I began the lecture, the audience's attitude changed, and now after every lecture I receive orders for at least the next 2 talks. As a teacher, I find it interesting to conduct such systematic teaching experiments. (03.02.1937)

Never is Vangenheim's courage more evident than in his correspondence with or about his daughter, Eleonora, or as her father often called her in his letters, Zvezdochka or Elchonka.

Where else can I look? Where else can I direct my thoughts? All seems gloomy, disquieting and in many ways, hopeless. My home, with those dear and beloved to me, is my only source of light and joy – it is the star that lights my way. And this gives me renewed strength and keeps me from losing heart, despite the terrible facts of grim reality. (18.02.1936)

Jewellery box with inkwell, 1934.

. . . When I have a spare minute I fashion pictures out of
stones on wood. I received permission to send you the
first example of my handiwork – I am making jewellery
boxes for Ellie. [. . .] I will send it as soon as I am able.
This work is good for my nerves. It distracts me a little
from my cumbersome thoughts and soothes me. All of
the stones on the jewellery box are from Popov Island,
and I have added bricks and coal stones too. I shall try to
identify each of the stones so that the jewellery box can
also serve as a mineral collection. I have already begun
work on the second one. (25.06.1934)

The majority of the letters that arrived in Moscow from
Solovki had been written on four pages torn from an exercise
book. On the lower quarters of the third and fourth pages,
Vangenheim would address drawings and notes to Eleonora,
thereby creating an ingenious and highly unusual textbook
for his pre-kindergarten daughter. It comprised sections on
botanical maths, plants and weather, mushrooms, berries, birds
and wild animals, riddles and natural phenomena.

I am currently overloaded with work due to the
cataloguing of the library, but it is not beyond my strength.

I have very little time to read, however, and have even had
to put off darning my socks until my day off. I have had
a few minutes every day to do something for Elchonka
though. I am sending her some puzzles now. It would be
good if someone could carefully explain to her the idea
behind the riddles and show her how to use the pictures.
I will compose several for her. (30.11.1934)

I have been intermittently attempting to draw a picture
for Elchonka – it is a view of the sea, as seen from my
window. I am sending two views of the same White Sea
bay. The picture of the sea with the purple nebulous
haze – a very distinctive phenomenon – has not quite
worked. But I think it is excusable, considering that this
is the first time in my life that I have used watercolour
paints. Perhaps I will practise and my efforts will improve.
Varyusha, give these pictures to Elchonka, my darling
Zvezdochka. (06.02.1934)

Seeking to educate his daughter, the father-cum-teacher also
amassed a herbarium of plants from Solovki. He placed dried
leaves in an envelope for her, drew the birds and animals that
inhabited the islands, and explained and illustrated the Northern
Lights, solar eclipses, the sea, and the island itself. Thus began the
process of the little girl's 'remote education' in the fundamentals
of mathematics, environmental sciences, geography and folklore.
As an experienced specialist teacher, Vangenheim always adapted
his lessons as his 'little student' grew older. His methods of
education were playful, but they also compelled one to think.

My darling little daughter! I am sending you two
mushrooms, types I have never seen myself: Milk-
white brittlegill (a tough, somewhat dry although
edible mushroom), and a truffle. This mushroom lives

Letters to his daughter, Ellie.

Ellie's Riddles. What lies still when alive but runs when it dies. (Answer – snow.)

underground, never revealing itself above the soil, and is
found with the help of pigs. The pigs rootle around in
the earth with their snouts, locate the mushrooms, and
a person retrieves them from directly under their noses.
I have drawn one truffle as a whole, and the other divided
in half; its centre is almost white. You must write and
tell me how many mushrooms you received. I sent them
today – 30. Write, my darling! Give our dear Mama a big
kiss. Your loving father is sending you lots of big kisses.
(31.10.1934)

The priest and philosopher Pavil Florensky, a fellow prisoner
at the camp, was so struck by Vangenheim's teaching efforts that
he wrote the following lines home:

An acquaintance of mine here has created a herbarium
of leaves for his daughter in order to teach her how to
count . . . he furnished this herbarium with names and
biological details. It would be good if Tika and Anya were
to create one of their own and give a few copies to their
school.

During his time at Solovki, Alexei Vangenheim developed
a serious case of neuralgia, which lost him the use of his left
hand. After spending two months in the camp hospital, he was
assigned to a team for the handicapped and sent to work in
the camp library, where he fulfilled the roles of guard, cleaner
and librarian combined. On top of this, and entirely of his own
volition, Vangenheim worked tirelessly to launch what he
referred to as his 'cultural-political initiatives'. He artistically
combined plants and stones of various colours to create
flowerbeds displaying red stars, Soviet symbols, and slogans such
as *Labour is a matter of honour* and *Correction*. He also created

portraits of Lenin and Dzerzhinsky* out of glass and stone, used Indian ink to draw portraits of Stalin, Sergei Kirov and Valerian Kuybyshev† on glass, and curated an exhibition in honour of the 15th Party Congress. Besides this, he contributed articles to the newspaper wall and took part in gatherings of the inmate-journalists responsible for the camp news board, for which he was awarded a signed copy of a book.

In September 1936, Vangenheim became manager of a museum in a section of the fortified former Solovki kremlin.‡ Vangenheim essentially founded the museum himself, having become its resident scientist, guard, cleaner and coal heaver. Letters from 1936–7 provide an account of his work there.

> At present I am very, very busy. Indeed, the work in the museum, my previous work in the library and the lectures all fall upon my shoulders. I have been required to clean up an internal area measuring 1,110 square metres in time for the celebration day, and to ensure that around 10,000 exhibits are dust-free. I have also been obliged to learn the full layout of the museum, so as to be able to lead excursions . . .

> I have familiarised myself with most of the material, although it is not entirely straightforward . . . I study literature in the intervals between cleaning, opening doors, stoking the stove and so on . . .

---

* Felix Dzerzhinsky was director of the first two Soviet security agencies, the Cheka and the OGPU, until his death in 1929. He is considered to be one of the architects of the Red Terror: the murder of hundreds of thousands of citizens considered to be 'anti-Bolshevik'.
† Valerian Kuybyshev was a highly influential Soviet political figure and principal economic advisor to Joseph Stalin.
‡ Translator's note: A monastery was established in the citadel in the fifteenth century but it was closed following the Bolshevik Revolution and many of its buildings were later incorporated into the labour camp.

For the last few days, with the exception of weekends,
I have been required to lead almost daily excursions . . .
there are sufficient exhibits, beginning with 16th-century
icons and wood carvings dating back as far as the 15th
century.

I am currently studying the history of war in order to
open a special department in one of the Kremlin towers
that has been allocated to us.

It has been necessary to devote special attention to the
question of old military munitions in setting up the
'Monastery as a Military Fortress' department.

At the moment, I am drawing up material for the
monastery's Economics department. I organised a lecture
by a specialist on sculpture for the study of the examples
in our possession and assisted him in his preliminary
classification of the exhibits. I am also working on a plan
to reorganise the Religious and Art History Departments,
for which I am reading a great many books . . .

The displays have developed to such an extent that rather
than taking 1 hour and 20 minutes, I now have to spend
3.5 – 4 hours on excursions, keeping explanations to
an absolute minimum. In a few days I will unveil the
'Solovki medicine' exhibition with its wonders, holy
water and other such baloney . . .

In this way, Vangenheim 'built socialism' at Solovki. He built
it the only way he knew: motivated by his conscience, rather
than a sense of fear. There were rewards for his 'strike labour',*

---

* The term 'strike labour' (*udarniy trud*) comes from the Russian *udarnik*, a
word coined in the Soviet Union during the first five-year plan to denote

but their benefits were limited to the confines of Solovki.

His letters outline a system of prisoner incentives:

- The ability to choose cellmates: *As a reward for carrying out my community workload I have been permitted to choose people with whom to share a room. We now live in a four: 3 serious working men and 1 youth, who I would like to set on the right path and encourage to study. Our quarters are a little cramped, but this is our choice . . .* (14.07.1934)
- The ability to receive *extra antiscorbutic rations.*
- The right to send more than the four letters he was permitted per month: *Today the new list of strike labourers was drawn up. I have remained on the list, so it follows that I can hope to send extra letters in March. Perhaps I will receive another 3, as has been the case for each of the last few months.* (24.02.1935)
- The right to purchase extra goods at the camp stall: *As a result of my work I have recently been awarded the right to buy a few things at the camp stall − socks, handkerchiefs and gloves; . . . I have earned the right to buy 500g of 'little pillow' humbugs at the camp stall.* (09.04.1935)
- An increase in food rations: *Now even material conditions are much better. While I was receiving Ration type 1 and 500g of bread, I had to cook for myself every day from personal food supplies. Now I receive Ration type 2; 800g of bread . . .* (11.11.1936)
- A higher wage for work: *For the past few months I have received a very high wage − 20 roubles per month. Compared with my previous salary of 1 rouble and 34 kopeks, this is an enormous leap.* (08.12.1935)
- A several day reduction in the length of a prison sentence as a reward for strike labour: *Working days for the third quarter were recently deducted. I had 31 days deducted for 3 months' work. You were interested in these numbers. I have 19 days for 1934, but for some reason I was only given my allowance for 3 of the 4 quarters*

---

a super-productive worker who put in hours above and beyond the norm, or generated above-average outputs due to his efficiency.

Botanical mathematics.

— 31 days each. So far nobody has been able to tell me why I was given nothing for the first quarter. For 1936 I have 3 quarters of 31 days each. It follows that I have accumulated a little more than 6 and a half (months), if this has not changed. Of course, it is a mere drop in the ocean. I am thankful, however, that they have even given me this. (16.10.1936)

But Vangenheim was not destined to be freed. On 9 October 1937, the creator of Solovki socialism was sentenced to death on the orders of a Troika of NKVD for the Leningrad region. He was charged with having an affiliation to the 'All-Ukrainian Central Block', a bourgeois-nationalist organisation allegedly operating within the camp. The sentence was carried out on the 3 November 1937 — Vangenheim was shot on the mainland at Sandarmokh.*

Eleonora Vangenheim writes in an afterword in the book *The Return of the Name Alexei Feodosevich Vangenheim*:

At the time of my father's arrest I was not yet four years old, so only a few distinctive episodes from our family life have remained lodged in my memory. My mother deserves huge credit for the fact that my father's letters were preserved. I remember them from my early childhood. Whenever they arrived, my mother would read them aloud — of course, she only read out the lines addressed to me. Afterwards she would carefully and deliberately hide the letters away for many years.

Right up until 1956, when the word 'posthumous' started appearing in enquiries about rehabilitation, my mother still hung on to the hope that my father was

---

* A large forested site in the Karelia region of Russia now known to have been an NKVD killing field. Excavations suggest that between 7,000 and 9,000 people were shot and buried in mass graves here between 1937 and 1938.

alive, and she waited for him to return. If I did something wrong, she would say, 'Soon your father will be back, and you will feel ashamed in front of him.' Measuring up to my father became my life's work and my mother developed and oversaw a programme of civic education that had been founded by him. In one of his letters to her, he had written: 'Let us hope that our daughter develops into as devoted a worker as you and I have been. Pass on my enthusiasm to her.' I would like to hope that I have at least fulfilled this particular wish of my father's.

Eleonora Vangenheim (1930–2012) graduated from the Geological Faculty of Moscow State University and became a Doctor of Geological Sciences. She initially worked as head of research in the Department of Palaeontology in the Geological Institute at the Russian Academy of Sciences before specialising in the field of animal palaeontology. She studied fossilisation in mammals and later became one of the country's leading mammoth experts.

Mikhail Bodrov

'Your incorrigible Trotskyist father'

Mikhail Bodrov was born into a peasant family in 1902 and he grew up on the outskirts of Moscow. From 1919 to 1923 he served in the Red Army and following his demobilisation he lived in Moscow, working until 1928 as a handyman for the Central Union of Consumer Societies, the supreme coordinating body of consumer cooperatives. In 1924 he married Vera Utkina – a woman from a neighbouring village – and brought her with him to Moscow. Their daughter, Tamara, was born in 1925, followed by a son, Anatoly, in 1927. But Bodrov's family life was to be short-lived: it came to an abrupt end with his first arrest in 1929.

Vera spoke very little to her children of their father, concealing the fact that he had been repressed and leading both them and the extended family to believe that he had drowned. It is possible that this was initially part of a conspiratorial plot of some kind. At any rate, we learn from Bodrov's letters that in 1934 Vera visited him in exile in Kazakhstan, though she never breathed a word of this to her children. Their daughter remembers only that, in her mother's words, 'Father was a very decent, honest man.' Vera would recount a time when she and Bodrov had been renting a bed in a communal Moscow apartment, not yet able to afford their own home. When the Central Union offered Bodrov a room of his own, he refused, offering it instead to a friend with two children, whom he deemed to be in greater need. This he did despite the fact that his own wife was pregnant, and it was to be some time before they received a room of their own on Razgulyay Square.

Bodrov became a member of the All-Union Communist Party (the Bolsheviks) in 1920, but just seven years later he was expelled on the grounds of having an 'affiliation with the Trotskyist opposition'.*

Prison photographs, 1929.

There can be no question that Mikhail Bodrov was a committed Trotskyist. When filling out his arrest forms upon his detention in June 1929 he made absolutely no attempt to conceal his political stance. He wrote:

> I completely and wholeheartedly stand in defence of the platform of opposition. I consider action of any form by

---

* The active persecution of 'Trotskyist opposition', to which Bodrov fell victim, began after the 14th convention of the All-Union Soviet Party in December 1927. The convention saw the approval of the expulsion from the party of Leon Trotsky and Grigory Zinovyev (a Bolshevik revolutionary and Soviet Communist politician) in addition to around one hundred of their supporters.

the opposition in the current situation to be absolutely necessary and will carry it out in any way possible. I believe the politics of the Russian Communist Party (Bolsheviks) to be wrong. I refute any reports that I had a role in, or acted in connection with or on behalf of the Bolshevik organisation.

Furthermore, in a letter that was intercepted by the NKVD, he wrote from his place of incarceration: 'Towards this detestable regime with which I have nothing in common I feel only vehement loathing, and I find myself in relentless contention with it.'

Mikhail Bodrov did not limit himself to making ideological announcements about his political views. By the age of twenty-seven he had become an active member of the Trotskyist underground movement and over the course of several months in 1928 he carried out a mission crucial to the opposition's cause. Secretly, and operating under a pseudonym, he transported clandestine correspondence from an exiled Trotsky in Alma Ata, covering over two hundred kilometres on horseback to Frunze* which marked the limit of the railway network, where he would hand over a message to another courier. Trotsky's own testimonials attest to the sheer scale of this operation:

> We sent around 800 political letters from Alma Ata, among which numbered several of great significance. Further to this, approximately 650 telegrams were sent. We received over 1,000 political letters, both long and short, and around 700 telegrams, most of which were from groups of people. For the most part, all of this correspondence was conducted while I was in exile. Besides these letters and telegrams, we also received 8 or 9 secret messages from Moscow; namely conspiratorial material delivered by couriers. Each one was answered. The secret Moscow

---

* Today Bishkek.

postal system kept me absolutely up to date with all goings-on and enabled me to react to the most important events with only the slightest delay.*

According to his comrades, Bodrov carried out this exceptionally risky operation admirably. The following excerpt is taken from an article written about him several years later in *The Opposition Bulletin*:[†]

A Moscow worker who served in the Red Army during the Civil War and a Bolshevik-Leninist. In the early months of 1928, after the exile of L. Trotsky to Alma Ata, comrade M. Bodrov was sent by the organisation to Alma Ata in order to maintain the communication network between L. Trotsky and Moscow. Having grown a beard and adopted the guise of a peasant from the Ural region, Bodrov acquired horses and carts to transport correspondence from Alma Ata to the nearest railway station (in Frunze; at least 200 versts)[‡] and back, disguised as a coachman. Comrade Bodrov demonstrated great tenacity, composure and adroitness in extremely challenging circumstances. He handled his responsibilities superbly, and facilitated Trotsky's link with Moscow under the most difficult circumstances. Approximately one year later, Comrade Bodrov was arrested in connection with other 'matters', whereupon he was also 'exposed' in his role as coachman. After spending many months in various prisons, Comrade Bodrov was finally exiled. Arrested once again, he was imprisoned for three years . . . Today he is in exile, or according to other sources, in a concentration camp.

---

* Trotsky archive in the Houghton Library at Harvard University, United States. Doc. bMs Russ 13 T-3149.
† *The Opposition Bulletin*, No.50, May, 1936. This bulletin was the official print mouthpiece of Trotskyist opposition. It was published in Paris between 1929 and 1941. Trotsky remained the editor of the publication until his death in 1940.
‡ A Russian unit of distance equating to approximately 1.07km.

Bodrov's last year of freedom was 1928, and it was perhaps the happiest of his life. On his return to Moscow in June 1929 he was arrested and, when searched, he was found to be carrying two photographs of Trotsky, a copy of Lenin's Testament and 'subversive' literature. This was his first arrest, and he was sent to the Chelyabinsk *Politisolator*.* Several further arrests, each on the grounds of 'anti-revolutionary Trotskyist activity', were to follow: in 1930, 1933 and 1935. During Bodrov's interrogations, the police demanded that he name his associates and sought to make him condemn Trotskyism. In response, he ostensibly declared his rejection of Trotskyism but not for a moment did he consider naming a single one of his comrades. Nor was he prepared to label Trotskyism an anti-Soviet movement.

In an extract from an interrogation record of 14 June 1930 Bodrov says:

> I declare that I have not conversed with any supporters of the Trotskyist opposition on the subject of the renewal or continuation of illegal activity. Since my return from political prison I have neither received nor read any illegal Trotskyist material and I know nothing about it. I cannot label the past activities and views of the opposition as counter-revolutionary.

Such a 'confession' was bound to give rise to further arrests. During a search upon his second arrest in 1935 Bodrov was found to be carrying an incriminating leaflet written in his own hand. The sharply critical tone of opposition was unmistakeable:

1. The Stalinist regime of the present day has absolutely nothing in common with the dictatorship of the proletariat, i.e. the

---

* Political isolation prisons run by the GPU-OGPU that operated between 1920 and the early 1930s. They were used to imprison anybody that the authorities considered to be 'political'.

power of the workers. In lieu of power to the workers we have an unrestricted dictatorship of bureaucratic oligarchs who, with their regime of terror, surpass both the former tsarist regime and even the governmental regimes of Germany and Italy.

2. Russia's working class are politically repressed and economic-ally exploited. Materially speaking, standards of living for Russia's workers are not only worse than Western Europe's unemployed population, but even those of Chinese coolies.

3. The term 'socialism' currently embodies nothing but lies and deceit.

4. The collective farming venture has wrought devastation upon the countryside.

5. A state of lawlessness reigns across the entire country. Prisons, places of exile and concentration camps are overflowing with hundreds of thousands of people guilty of absolutely nothing at all.

6. The powers-that-be gorge themselves without restraint while beneath them the working masses and toiling peasants collapse from starvation and their back-breaking labour.

7. In cities, in factories and plants, in villages and collective and state farms, work systems evoke recollections of serfdom.*

A statement from the records of the Special Board of NKVD dated 20 June 1935 reads:

> Mikhail Bodrov was sent to Semipalatinsk, where he lived until the end of 1934. He worked as an economist for the Regional Demand Procurement Agency. He maintained regular correspondence with his Trotskyist comrades and in 1935 was arrested again by the NKVD, in East Kazakhstan. He was charged in accordance with Articles 58-10 and

---

* V. Veikhman, 'Will the Old Commander Rise Again?' A short story (Tel Aviv: Ivrus), 2002.

58-11 of the Penal Code of the Russian Soviet Federated Socialist Republic with carrying out systematic counter-revolutionary propaganda campaigns and inciting agitation among the population in the city of Semipalatinsk, as well as seeking to instil Trotskyist beliefs in easily led communist citizens, organising fundraising, and attempting to send illegal letters containing his counter-revolutionary messages to Moscow.

Following his final arrest, Bodrov was sentenced to five years in a labour camp. He was initially sent to the Karlag in Kazakhstan, before being moved to the Sevvostlag in Kolyma. Here, on account of his status as a 'particularly dangerous' individual, he was transferred to a separate site in the small village of Zyryanka, just 90 kilometres from the Arctic Circle. In his narrative essay 'Will the Old Commander Rise Again?', Vladimir Veikhman writes:

No matter where he found himself, Mikhail Bodrov was forever instigating protest movements. At the Karagandinskaya transit point he . . . organised a demonstration against biased investigations. The trains transporting the prisoners to Karagandinskaya stopped off in Krasnoyarsk, and here he sent a sharply critical statement to the NKVD on behalf of all the political prisoners. En route to Vladivostok, Bodrov declared to the regional public prosecutor who was trying to persuade the prisoners to travel on the Kulu ship: 'All of the NKVD's actions are sheer self-serving provocation — their sole aim is to get us onto the steam ship.'*

---

* Translator's note: From the late 1930s to early 1950s, hundreds of thousands of prisoners were shipped to Kolyma, loaded into extremely cramped holds and often forced to lie on the bed-boards for the entire two to three week voyage. The holds of these 'slave ships' (as described by Martin Bollinger in his book

As Veikhman reports in his story, informers were rife among the political prisoners:

> Source: Botfly
> Received: Ivanov
> 12/07/1936
> Agent Report
>
> Several organisers of counter-revolutionary activity boarded the Kulu. They were Trotskyists and called themselves 'Starostats'.* Without any formal elections they appointed the following individuals as the leaders of their counter-revolutionary activities: Bodrov, Baranovsky, Sayansky and Martov. At the Sevvostlag quarantine point, these individuals mustered Trotskyist supporters around them and incited unrest, attracting other prisoners to their sides by saying that we were being taken to Kolyma to be killed. They encouraged the men to follow their example and take up the fight against the organs of the NKVD.

In a speech made by Mikhail Bodrov to a group of political exiles he said:

> You, Comrades, do not see what is taking place beneath your very noses. There is no dictatorship of the proletariat, but rather a Bonaparte-Fascist dictatorship. The party is witnessing a Thermidor and not even a trace of the guiding lines of Leninism remains. It consists solely of officials who carry out Stalin's latest orders.

Stalin's Slave Ships: Kolyma, the Gulag Fleet, and the Role of the West) were often kept covered so that foreign ships and aeroplanes would not be able to see the cargo.

* Starostats were the unofficial governing organs for political prisoners at Solovki and other detention facilities for political prisoners. They acted as prisoner representatives for negotiation with the camp administration, among other things.

Mikhail Bodrov was one of the chief initiators of the hunger strike of 204 Trotskyist prisoners at the Magadan quarantine point. We know that his relationship with the camp authorities had become extremely hostile, and both his surname and that of his civil partner, Anisiya Shtifanova, featured constantly in secret service reports. Bodrov refused to work and described attempts to interfere in his personal relationships as 'vile and shameless blackmail'. He added: 'As for the overt threats of punishing my refusal to work with a reduction in my food rations, I find this merely facetious and amusing. The notion of "frightening" a political prisoner imprisoned unremittingly since 1929 with the threat of reduced rations is simply not smart.'

Imprisoned in a labour camp in the hopeless backwater of Zyryanka (Kolyma), Bodrov continued to stick stubbornly to his principles, albeit resorting to increasingly desperate methods. When he was moved to the tent for prisoners under guard as a result of his refusal to work, Veikhman writes that Bodrov, 'made a small cut in his neck with the blade of a razor'. Shtifanova is said to have shrieked, 'Misha, wait! Be strong! You must show the other workers how to deal with these fascists!'

While incarcerated at Kolyma, Bodrov continued to play an active role in the camp opposition and he is reported to have taken part in a large-scale labour dispute carried out by the Trotskyist inmates in the form of another hunger strike. The ending was inevitable. Following the resolution of a Troika of NKVD for the USVITlag* on 14 September 1937, Bodrov was sentenced to death. He was shot shortly afterwards.

Twenty-five letters penned by Mikhail Bodrov have been collected and filed in Memorial's archives. Of these letters, twenty-four are addressed to his opposition comrades and one to his seven-year-old son, Tolya:

---

* Directorate of the NKVD North-Eastern Corrective Labour Camps.

To my sweet little Tolya,

I am sending you a notebook as a memento – it is one that I received while still in prison. Use it for your lessons. When you have filled it up, keep it as a reminder that your father spent about five years in prison. When we meet, I will use it to assess your very first steps as a student. Study just as well as your sister Tamarochka.

I am sending you a big kiss.

Your incorrigible Trotskyist father,

M. Bodov

From Semipalatinsk – in exile (05.10.1934)

Tolya never read his father's letter. Sadly, not one of the letters from Bodrov in Memorial's possession arrived at its intended address – the NKVD intercepted every single one. It is likely that Bodrov had tried to give them to his wife when she came to visit him in exile in Kazakhstan, but that the NKVD seized them. In the end they were filed in his NKVD case dossier and only brought to light in 1995 by employees of Memorial.

Mikhail Bodrov's son, Anatoly, became an engineer and died in the 1960s. His daughter, Tamara, studied typewriting and stenography before volunteering for the front during the war, where she worked at Army Headquarters. She later went on trade missions to Bucharest with the USSR Ministry of Foreign Trade. Tamara considered her father to be a true communist. She died in 1995 but is survived by a daughter, Larisa Obanicheva, who lives in Paris and provided much of the information on her grandfather, as well as photographs from his case file.

Моему милому мальчику - Толе!

Посылаю тебе на память тетрадь, которую я получил еще будучи в тюрьме.

Записывай в нее свои уроки. Когда испишешь - сохрани, как память, что твой папа около пяти лет просидел в тюрьме.

Когда мы встретимся с тобою, по записям в этой тетради - я буду судить о твоих первых ученических шагах.

Учись так-же хорошо, как хорошо учится твоя сестрица - Тамарочка.

Крепко целую тебя.

Твой неисправимый троцкист папа

М Бодров

г. Семипалатинск - ссылка

5/X-34.

The only surviving letter written by Mikhail Bodrov to his son, 5 October 1934.

Yevgeny Yablokov

'I believe in our children'

Yevgeny Yablokov, a teacher of botany at Ryazan Pedagogical University, was arrested by the NKVD on 10 January 1938 and sent to a labour camp in the Arkhangelsk region, from where he wrote letters home to his family. Sentenced to eight years' imprisonment, he died from malnutrition and illness in March 1944. A remarkable 294 letters from Yablokov (including postcards) have been preserved.

Yevgeny Ivanovich Yablokov, Ryazan, 1935.

They are addressed to his wife, Nina, and their children: a daughter, Irina, who was fifteen at the time of her father's arrest, and a son, Yuri, who saw his father for the last time at the age of just eleven. In his memoirs Yuri writes:

> It is thanks to my mother, Nina Yablokova, wife and faithful friend to my father (1894–1984), that his letters were preserved. When my mother moved from Ryazan to Moscow (in the mid-sixties), I collected and safeguarded the letters. Between 2004 and 2009, barring a few interruptions, I deciphered and typed them up. I had to use a magnifying

loupe to make the small handwriting legible; it was faded in places, and spotted with graphite from the pencil-written text. The paper was in poor condition from where it had been folded, and we had to enlarge some sections with a scanner and make use of computer reconstruction software to render certain parts legible. The organisation 'Memorial' in Moscow helped enormously in this endeavour.

The letters allow one to picture and begin to comprehend the real-life tragedy that my father undeservedly suffered. I believe that I owe it to him to preserve them for future generations, and I am pleased to have been able to do so.

Up until 1938 there had been nothing in the life of Yevgeny Yablokov to signal a tragic turning of the tide. He was born in Ryazan in 1887 into the family of a civil servant who had risen to the rank of State Councillor. Before the Revolution, Yablokov studied in both St Petersburg and Lyon. He graduated from Moscow University with 'the right to teach at gymnasiums and progymnasiums in the subjects of Natural Sciences and Geography' and went on to teach botany at a Moscow gymnasium.

After the October Revolution, his father fell ill and he returned to Ryazan, where he took up a teaching post at an agricultural training college. In 1921 he married a nurse he had known since childhood and two years later their daughter was born, followed by a son two years after that. Before long, Yablokov had been appointed as an associate professor at the Ryazan Pedagogical Institute.

In January 1938 he was due to begin defending his Candidate of Sciences* thesis on the propagation of rice crops in the north. But the thesis went unfinished: Yablokov was arrested in the middle of the night on 10 January. The arrest followed a conflict

---

* The Candidate of Sciences (*kandidat nauk*) was introduced in the USSR in 1934 and is considered to be a qualification equivalent to the PhD.

The Yablokov family, Ryazan, late 1920s.

with the director of the teaching institute who, wishing to install a person of his choice in Yablokov's place, had issued an order for his dismissal. Yablokov resisted, and though the People's Commissariat of Education eventually concluded that he should be reinstated in his original position, the conflict was never truly resolved. Yablokov is quoted in the interrogation records dated 20 January 1938 as saying, 'I consider the events of the past two months at the teaching institute, of which this arrest is a direct consequence, to constitute unjustified harassment.'

In his memoirs Yuri Yablokov writes:

> From as early as November, my father's friends had been advising him to leave Ryazan right away. Judging by the job offers (most notably from Moscow's Botanical Gardens) that arrived after his arrest, he had contemplated heeding their advice, but only once he had been reinstated at work following his unwarranted dismissal. It is hard to say whether leaving Ryazan would have spared my father from arrest.

The official charge contrived by the NKVD appeared unrelated to the conflict at the teaching institute. Yablokov was accused of participation in a fictitious counter-revolutionary organisation. On learning more about his father's 'case', Yuri writes in his memoirs:

> The criminal report alleges that my father was a member of a counter-revolutionary organisation (Articles 58-10, 58-11), and that he was incriminated by the testimonies of other defendants . . . He denied the charges.
>
> . . .
>
> From my father's complaints to the procurator and the conversations he had with his wife between 26 and 28 July 1939, it is clear that he never had any idea which organisation he had been accused of having an affiliation with. We learn from the interrogation records that he vehemently denied false quotes derived from his lecture on the characteristics of plant succession. They did not adopt physical measures against him as a means of leverage, except for denying him access to the bathroom (which nevertheless constituted a form of torture for people like my father). More often than not, the investigator employed the 'trust' tactic, persuading my father to sign his name on a blank sheet of paper. He alleged that this would speed up the interrogation and promised to later write 'everything exactly as it was said'. Having been granted permission to review his case files, I can say with absolute certainty that my father incriminated neither himself, nor anybody else during his interrogation. The only people that he listed as acquaintances were his colleagues at the teaching institute, with whom it was inevitable that he would have communicated. He did not mention a single friend or relative . . . I was unable to find in the report any grounds for his conviction, but I was not given access to all of the files, owing to the fact that his was

allegedly a 'group' case. Of the six reports allegedly signed by my father, only one signature seemed genuinely authentic.

As soon as the inquest was over and he had embarked on the long journey to his new place of imprisonment, Yablokov began to write letters home. He addressed separate letters, or individual parts of them to his wife, daughter and son. In one letter to his wife he writes:

> I believe in our children; Irusya is a good, sweet girl with a wonderful character and great potential. I believe in Yurik's potential too and know that his good qualities will help him to achieve it. I will write, and hope that I can keep in touch and be of help to them. The letters must arrive in time, before I grow too old. (28.06.1938)

Yablokov suggested games and books, and helped where he could with his children's studies and later on their choices of profession. All the while, he offered his own moral evaluations of life's different circumstances and characters. He explained his personal opinions on good and evil, on justice and injustice, and shared his dreams for a future in which he would be back home again. The following are a few extracts from letters he wrote to his children:

> To Yuri:
> When I dreamed of my future release, I imagined how you and I will go fishing – I have learned [. . .] a new way of catching fish. I also dreamed of how you and I will take turns to help your mother and Irusya with the chores. At least two days in six* we will help your mother to cook lunch and go to buy the groceries.

---

* Six-day working weeks were the norm in the Soviet Union at this time.

To Ira:

My joy, my daughter. Thank you for trying so hard
at school and in your music lessons. Back when I was
being held in Ryazan, I dreamed of how I would read
through everything that you are studying on nature and
geography, and help you by explaining the things that I
know.

To Yuri:

Live happily, my darling, and be good . . . Love your
mother, love Irusya, and by that I mean be good to them.
[. . .] I remember how your tenderness set you apart from
others when you were little. This shows that you had, and
still have, the gift of love and warmth. You must nurture
this gift through doing good.

To Ira:

Congratulations on reaching the end of your seventh
year at school, and not just that, but for achieving such
good grades and earning a prize – a book by Shchedrin.*
You may find it a little difficult to read, but I urge you to
finish it. I would have read it with you . . .

To Ira:

All the same, Geography is a good subject. Study, and you
will not regret it. Find a way to read some geographical
anthologies – you can pick up a few at the library. You
might look up the following authors: 1) Nosilova (small,
thin); 2) Nechaeva, On Land and Sea; 3) Krubert,
Grigorieva, Geography (several thick books). Or find
some other newer publications . . .

---

* Presumably here Yablokov is referring to a book by the famous nineteenth-
century Russian satirist Mikhail Saltykov-Shchedrin.

To Yuri:

My sweet, sweet boy. Thank you for your postcard and for your promise of sending 'more details' in a letter. I noticed how painstakingly you had written . . . You wrote well. I am very pleased that you have started the year with good grades . . .

To Ira:

I am very, very pleased that my parcel containing the dried plants arrived.

To Ira:

Some time ago we took a steamboat to Pinega and witnessed a rare sight; I forgot to write about it for you and Yuri. A leveret hopped away from the water up the steep bank – it must have come there to drink. Suddenly, an owl appeared above it and we saw it lower its legs and stretch out its talons. It flapped its wings above the leveret, which suddenly noticed it, and, standing on its back legs, waved its front paws to defend itself. All would have ended badly, had the ship not let out a whistle – I assume on purpose so as to frighten the owl, which flew away, alarmed. The little leveret ran away up the hillside. This entire episode lasted only a minute and yet writing about it takes so long.

To Ira:

A few days ago it occurred to me to suggest that you and Yuri write a story describing the owl attack on the leveret that I wrote about in my letter. Let's do it together, all three of us: You, Yuri and I will each write a story and send it to the editors of 'The Young Naturalist'. It will be our competition, and the editors will be the panel of judges.

To Yuri:

My son, my Yura, I received your postcard and will
await your letter. Yesterday I wrote to Irusya and asked
her about your essay, but today I found out from you
that it was a success. Nevertheless, I would like to know
more about the essay, and to know which wall newspaper
published it. Let's just say, I would like some more
specific details, with examples . . .

To Ira:

It brings me such joy to hear about your achievements
in your studies and music, and to know that you are
particularly enjoying the sciences – Physics, Chemistry,
Mathematics [. . .] Among my books (I think it may be
in the kitchen, or on the bookshelf) are the following:
'Physics for Entertainment' by Perelman and 'Experiments
in Chemistry'. There ought too to be a book by Lassar-
Cohn called 'Chemistry in Daily Life'. Try to read these
books if you can locate them and find the time.

To Yuri:

12 years! Already so many! Now begins your conscious
experience, which will develop fully over the next 12
years. And when you reach 24 years of age you will start
to think that you have already lived your life and yet
you will feel that you have achieved nothing. Almost
everybody feels this way . . . so above all you must
study – go to school and get a primary, secondary and
higher education so as not to simply dream about what
it is you want to achieve, but to actually accomplish it.
And so, my sweet boy, I wish you success over the next
twelve years in all that I have mentioned; in the sciences,
in your conscious and perceptive development and in
your achievements (being able to realise your dreams is

essential). I dare say that what I am writing is boring and difficult to understand. So . . . read it a few times . . .

To Ira:
I find myself wanting to share all of my thoughts, or those that are in any way valuable, with you and Yuri. Perhaps they are not so significant or easy to convey and digest, but parts of them, those that I consider worthwhile, are important. I feel such a strong desire to share them with you.

To Ira:
Life has such wonderful potential, and yet so much of it is terrible. How can we come to terms with this contradiction? You don't need to come to terms with it; you need only understand that contradiction is a characteristic of the world; a feature of life. You must have faith, and every now and again everyone does feel, and believe, that life is wonderful. It is really only faith, faith in goodness, that saves us from despondency and sustains us.

   Yevgeny Yablokov continued to write his children letters such as these, permeated with love and tenderness, for the entire duration of his imprisonment – he wrote right up until the day he died. Reading them, one marvels at how candidly he spoke of his work and living conditions. In letters to his wife and children between 1938 and 1944, Yablokov shared many of the 'camp truths' that were later to emerge in the memoirs of former camp prisoners Alexander Solzhenitsyn and Yevgenia Ginzburg.* Naturally, much was omitted, and he always cast a cautious eye towards camp censorship. Yablokov was also careful

---

* Russian authors who served long sentences in the Gulag.

to spare the feelings of his wife and children when describing camp life, yet he nonetheless somehow managed to convey the truth. He wrote about his work as a tree feller and timber rafter, about camp gruel and life alongside criminals, and about illnesses brought on by hunger, cold and malnutrition.

My sweet son Yura,

Today I turned 51 years old [. . .]
I got up at 5 a.m.; an hour earlier than we are woken. The sun had risen, although there was no darkness anyway as it was light all night. I love mornings best of all; the earlier the hour, the better they look . . . I get up early so as not to have to rush (everything here is done hurriedly you see), not only over breakfast, but also my cup of tea – your mother sends me enough that I can drink it three times a day. I wake up early to reread your old or recent letters, and once I have read them I yearn to write to you, but by then there is too little time. Once in a while I manage to write a postcard; those I always write in the mornings, but letters I write in the evenings or at night . . .
[. . .] And so, at 7 o' clock in the morning we leave for 'allocation' – by this I mean that each brigade receives their instructions and heads off to work. My brigade (I am in a new one – 'Voronin') goes to float timber at the processing mill, which lies at the confluence of the Pinega and Northern Dvina rivers. Our camp is right on the bank of the Northern Dvina. We walk along the bank, carrying our boathooks, for about half a kilometre until we reach the Pinega confluence. There we must take a sailing boat across to the opposite bank, but at present the right hand side of the Pinega is very shallow so we have to wade across to the bank – the water comes to

below the knee. Next we walk along the 'bon' ('bon' is the name we give to the floating rafts consisting of three logs joined together). It stretches out across the river for around 100 metres and then lengthways for a few hundred metres forming an entire system, so to speak, of waterways with canals and pockets leading up to the processing mill, which also connects the rafts. I will draw a picture to help you understand:

Explanation of the drawing:

1. The processing mill is on the right. The mechanism is fuelled by electrical energy, which gathers the floating logs together into 'bundles' and ties them up with wire into rafts (about 150–400 logs depending on their size)

2. The entire picture (and all of the lines) is drawn on the surface of the river. There is one machine on the Pinega and two identical ones on the Northern Dvina. I have not drawn the people, but they are everywhere:

    a) at the processing mill – in the hut on the platform.

    b) on every little bridge, at the gates (the bridges must be accessed from both sides). Everybody holds a boat-hook.

3. The water flows, and the logs float down the river – at first they are all over the place. The closer they get to the

processing mill, the better they align with the canals and
move into bundles, side by side.

4. Various types of wood material collect in the pockets
(arranged according to species, thickness and purpose).

5. People sort a continuous body of timber, pushing
it along to be separated into the canals or 'pockets'.
Eventually it ends up at the processing mill.

. . . I have drawn a very condensed picture of the sorting
system; in actual fact the 'pockets' are far more numerous
– there are up to 13 of them, a figure proportional to
the different varieties of forest material. Besides this
you need to imagine that a large amount of wood
accumulates in disarray before it arrives at the start of the
sorting system. You could say that this area becomes a
'general pocket' and we call it the 'holding zone'. When
the wood accumulates and is carried down from either
of the tributaries, its movement is interrupted by the
'bons' and the logs pile up against one another so that
they cannot move any further. This blockage is called a
logjam, and it is necessary to break it up straight away.
This is done by moving individual parts of the lumber,
so that others can then slide past towards the 'main
gate', and from there they float on to be sorted. People
straighten them up and guide them along. I work at the
main gate itself, assisting in the 'breaking up and passage'
of the timber.

It was this very same morning (the one I began to
describe earlier) that I saw an Atlantic salmon for the first
time. We had been sent out to work and arrived at the
Pinega, where we found 2 rowing boats on the bank.
A fisherman sat in one, and I saw the fish that he had
caught. It was about 70–80cm long, silvery and speckled.
In order to walk across the bons you need to remove your

shoes. Your Mama had sent me some underpants (black) the day before and I, stripped down to just them and a shirt, got into the boat. To tell the truth, until then I had been wearing two pairs of warm trousers – both sleeping and working in them. It had been necessary to keep them safe you see, but things are better now, and belongings have almost stopped disappearing.

Our weather here is just as hot as it is with you. You and Irusenka asked me, 'Is the weather with you similar to ours?' Yes, I believe so. So it appears anyway, judging by the newspapers and your letters. We are used to the changeable weather of June, to the cold, and to the absolutely unbelievable and uncharacteristic heat of July. But the locals say that July and August are good summer months here. We shall see what the weather is like from here on. Yesterday it rained and we were soaked through at work immediately as there is nowhere to shelter. We soon dried out though – I work the morning shift, which meant that I was in the sun. There are three different shifts: from 12 p.m. until 8 a.m.; from 8 a.m. to 4 p.m.; from 4 p.m. to 12 midnight. The three groups work in shifts twenty-four hours a day. I too will have to work a different shift, as we will rotate in ten days' time. But night is as light as day here anyway.

A boat goes across to the sorting bon; all 40 people sitting in the sailing boat get out and disperse along the floating panels and bridges to occupy their respective positions. The work groups change over and there is time for a smoke before work begins. Then for 8 uninterrupted hours the river flows and the logs float down, people with boathooks constantly moving them with one end or other of their boathooks where necessary. There is no time to smoke; we are not permitted to take a break. Sometimes there is; when the logs stop floating down and some

people go to break them up, leaving the others with a
chance moment to rest. The sun burns down, but bathing
while at work is forbidden. That said, every once in a
while somebody loses their footing and slips into the water
before climbing out of their fortuitous bath. The sun is
scorching, and those who are careless strip off completely
at work and get burned; some are blistered, as though
burned by boiling water. I am very careful and work only
in my underwear, without shoes but wearing socks.

[. . .] Sometimes, rarely – not every day, aeroplanes fly
overhead. Every day beautiful white passenger ships steam
past along the Dvina. Oh, how I wish I could be on one
of those ships. There are also little tugboats pulling huge
rafts much longer than themselves.

In the greenery on the bank, out of sight but not out of
earshot, a husky dog barks at squirrels for hours on end.
People say that it will bark until nightfall, when it is taken
away. Do you remember how our Becky also used to
bark among the trees at Davidovka? She too must have an
innate squirrel-hunting instinct.

You grow very tired after standing for eight hours on
the water conveyor belt. Your hands swell from holding
on to the wooden boathooks and it is difficult to grip
them or to clench your fists. There are many joints in the
body, and each joint aches when it moves – when you
climb onto your bunk after work, for example . . .

But we ignore this.

Timber floating has been recognised by the
government as strike labour, and has been deemed of
equal importance to the Arkhangelsk region and our
country as the White-Sea Baltic Canal and the Moscow-
Volga Canal. If our camp can exceed the work norms and
finish the floating by 25.08 (on government orders), many
prisoners will be given privileges . . .

. . . Yesterday we had our general meeting of prisoners on the subject of Stakhanovite* timber floater of the month. Our work improved for the first five days after our start date of 15.07. Yesterday we received orders that we must speed up our efforts and finish not by the 25th, but by 15.08. Everybody is working well, and we all promise to work even harder – it would be good if we managed to meet this deadline. Many people have been promised a reduction in the length of their sentence and other such privileges. It is a pity that I have less strength than the younger men and I am simply unable to match them.

The work itself does not demand great strength or much movement; I need to turn the logs and pull them along dextrously with the boathook so that they do not cause a blockage by floating sideways across the canal. It is good to work on your feet when the weather is fine – we float above the water under the heat of the sun and have the chance to dip our feet in the water and to splash a little on our heads. It's just that the work demands careful attention and dexterity so it's very tiring. That said, the goal is great – they have promised to reward superproductive labour very generously, at least for many of the best and strongest workers.

But I must finish my letter, sweetheart. It's uncomfortably long. [. . .]

Your 'Pip' – who has grown old. (24.07.1938)

'My good little Irinochka and Yurik. [. . .]

I congratulate both of you on the spring warmth and air.

---

* Translator's note: The term 'Stakhanovite' refers to a worker in the Soviet Union who proved to be exceptionally hard-working and productive. The term was coined in 1935, when Aleksei Grigorievich Stakhanov mined 102 tonnes of coal in less than six hours, a quantity which was fourteen times greater than his quota. He became a Hero of the Soviet Union and inspired an eponymous movement designed to increase worker productivity.

The first plants are blooming here too – spurge laurel shrubs (Daphne meseraum). You can read about them in Tsinger's 'Engaging Botanics'.

As when I last wrote, I am still working in tree felling – we are pulling out roots and stumps, and burning them. The weather is good during the day – it has been like this for the last three days, but before that it was cold. Geese, cranes and swans continue to fly overhead. The logs and firewood are still being transported across the work area on sledges, even though there is no snow. They transport them across the ground like this:

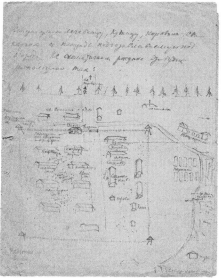

Sweethearts, this postcard-letter doesn't count; I am writing so as to reply quickly, but as soon as I have a day off I will write you a proper letter, although as well as this one (and the one I wrote on 11.04) you will have received another postcard (09.05) and one on 12.05. I am writing to thank you both for your letter, parcel, achievements, and for being my little darlings.

Your Papa, Yevgeny Yab[lokov] (17.05.1939)

I would like you to be able to imagine the layout of the place where I live. It is encircled by forest (to be more precise, the outline is 'square'), a forest of spruce and aspen, admittedly with birch trees and pines too. The spruces are not very old, but the aspens are extremely tall, with huge thick trunks. The pines are long and skinny . . . It is damp in the forest, and there are lots of lingonberries and bilberries growing among the moss. Apparently there are lots of raspberries here too . . . There are a great many dead trees whose trunks, covered in moss, are dying a natural death. Two or three clearings cut straight through the forest; one leads to the 'transfer' road (the road by which vehicles travel from Nyandoma to Kargopol) and the other extends towards the village and lake. The 'transfer' site is the place where whatever is being transported (people or material) is transferred from vehicles to horse-drawn transport. I believe that it is 24 km from Nyandoma to the transfer site, and 4 km from there to the logging camp.

The camp itself is situated in a square forest clearing, which encircles not only the zone containing the prisoners' barracks, but also the accommodation blocks for the administrators and free workers, which are just outside the camp zone. The agricultural homestead is also within this area so there are rows of agricultural buildings too: a greenhouse, seed germination beds, a cowshed, a pigsty and a plot of land that is being prepared for a vegetable garden.

There is a so-called camp intelligentsia here, composed of orderlies who work in the office and people from the camp administrative office – supervisors of household matters and medical workers etc. Their lives are easier and they are better dressed – they can wear their own clothes. Most of the prisoners work in 'production' (tree-felling, timber floating, agricultural work . . .). Our government-issue clothes are often dirty and we are out at work all day. I have come to understand what it is to live a life of physical labour: 12 hours on the job, and food before and after work. You are exhausted by the labour and the food, and crave sleep. And that's it: the physical life is comprised solely of muscle, food and sleep. Therefore if you subtract from 12 hours the time spent at work (and walking back), queuing for and collecting food, washing one's dishes, morning and evening 'toilette', caring for and drying out one's shoes, going to the washhouse and the camp stall etc., so little time remains that to waste it by simply lying about and listening to conversations or reading the paper results in nothing but a deficit of sleep. We are so exhausted that there is just no time for reading, writing, or even dozing. On a separate note, there are also women in our section of the camp. Firstly there are the 'mamas': this is what we call the young women who have children (some still babes-in-arms), whose familiar cries and screams you hear when passing their barracks. Secondly, there are the 'ladies', who dress as though living in the city, in fur coats (often expensive-looking) and generally wearing stylish suits. I have no idea who they were in the past and know only that there are accountants, teachers and other such professionals among them. As a result, the population of our camp station is around 1 thousand, and it is very diverse in terms of backgrounds, professions and appearances. To a certain extent, these other people invoke a strange impression of the 'intelligentsia', especially at camp 'concerts' and other such evening functions, but even just in the canteen! This wasn't the case in the labour colonies where there were only labourers and scores of common criminals. Here almost all of the prisoners are 'politicals', while there, a good many were so-called 'urki' (from *ugolovniy rozisk* = u-r = urki).* The people there were fiery, impudent, jovial, rude, vulgar, drunken and brawling, which set the tone for life in the colony. They were in particular need of 'corrective labour' and education, since they avoided all work in general. Here too, there are people who shirk work where possible. They have no fear of punishment and manage to earn a living through stealing and playing cards. But the tenor of life here in the camp is very different from that in the colonies. It is easier to live here – there seem to be many good people around. I know a few in my own brigade – farmers from the collectives, labourers and desk workers. (20.05.1939)

My sweet son, my Yuri,
Congratulations on the success of your school trip. I must admit that from your description I strongly approve of the way that it was organised. The schedule was wonderful and it was very sensibly planned. It was good that they allowed you to visit the Moscow Art Theatre independently. That was excellent.

Thank you for writing to me not only on the day you set off on the trip, but also when you returned. I hope that you have not exhausted your supply of details with all these descriptions? Will you tell me more about your trip in your letters to me, even though new events in your life will move in to take their place? I am interested to know what you bought for your study group and how and why you put these things to use. What thoughts did you have in the Planetarium? And also, of course, in the Tretyakov Gallery and Museum of Fine Arts? And the 'Blue Bird'?†

---

* A term derived from the words '*ugolovniy rozisk*' meaning 'criminal investigation'. Urki were common criminals; bandits and thieves.
† A play by Belgian playwright Maurice Maeterlinck.

You won't find it hard to write about this trip now, while you are still reliving it all among yourselves. Oh, I so want to hear about your meeting too. [. . .]

Rays of sunlight are falling across me as the sun rises; they come in over the top of the curtains, which are brightly coloured, like a sundress. This is only in our half of the barracks. Almost everybody is asleep, so it is a convenient time to look around and describe the room.

This is the layout [hand drawn picture]. There aren't many windows, but it is lit from two sides. It is clean, and we have linen and blankets on the beds. The scale of the picture does not enable me to show that the tables are strewn with chess pieces from the previous day's games and teapots full of hot water. I have already drunk some tea with a little bread and butter and sprats (which you sent me and I am trying for the first time. The sprats are very good.). I had a good night; in truth I did not sleep, but had some time to myself and wrote you a letter . . .

Lots of people play chess here because we hold a tournament – only for men from our barracks, but even so, there are 17 participants. I also play (moderately well) and think that I will probably be among the ten who play in the final round. I will let you know the results in a month's time.

In the little cupboard that hangs above my crib I keep my dishes, books, cooking pot, mug, glass, and tins containing sugar, sushki* and butter . . . Having started with nothing, it seems that I now have rather a lot [. . .]

I am working in the office as before, but it has been moved temporarily to a different building. A short-sided table stands by the window, and four of us sit behind it. I have put some branches with green leaves and birch

---

* Traditional Russian ring-shaped snacks made from water, egg, flour and salt.

catkins on the windowsill. Outside the window it is snowy and slushy, but today it is blizzarding (although to tell the truth it is not soft snow that is falling, but hard balls). This is what we expect during the transitional seasons of autumn and spring. I have just reread your two previous letters, not for the first time . . . and they are both interesting.

You wrote about Mishka, who is about to have kittens . . . Almost two months will have passed from the day that you wrote (04.03) to the day that you receive this letter, and the kittens will be quite a size. I dare say that Mishka will move them about from place to place, as is natural. People, and by that I mean all of you, will undoubtedly get in her way. But who is to know what it is that she needs most. Mishka doesn't act according to her own thinking, but to her innate instincts − perhaps they are prudent and entirely sound? You rarely mention Becky. Mama Nina writes only good things about her . . . about how she never leaves her side. Does Becky respond at all to the words, 'Where's Papa?'

A short time ago I had to spend a few days sawing firewood (for general work), and while doing so I repeatedly found myself thinking that I would like to saw wood with you, or with Nina. Actually, instead of sawing with her, I would rather do it myself with a bow saw. I tell you this to give you an idea of the thoughts evoked by certain phrases in your letters, and to show you that each one of your phrases gives rise to several different thoughts and wishes.

Perhaps Auntie Lida has already crossed the river and come to stay, and I imagine that she will listen to both your and Irusya's accounts of your excursion with wonder and fascination. Pass on my best wishes to her [. . .]

I am very grateful for the books that you sent and the

'Science and Life' journal, which I received in your latest parcel (30.03). I received it on the 10th, and the book came a little later, on the 20th, having been checked over. It contains many wonderful articles. What are you reading, other than short stories?

Thank you for all that you sent. It was only the meat that was covered with green mould, but I cleaned it off without difficulty and enjoyed it enormously. I already know about the purchases you and Irusya made for me – thank you my sweethearts . . . I expect that the next parcel will arrive either at the end of May or in early June.

Well, goodbye my sweethearts, my little darlings. From me – your father, Yevgeny. (Night, 27–28.04.1940)

My sweet little son, My Yuri!
I understand absolutely everything you say in your letters, especially the parts where you express your feelings. It is wonderful that you look forward to my letters, are getting on well with Irina and have received a letter from Verochka.

Winter is with us here; it began a long time ago, and came early (on 25.10). We have had ten days or more of good warm winter days, without blizzards and cold weather. Our snow might also be slightly too sticky to cross-country ski, although nobody from the camp goes skiing. Instead they complain about getting wet in the deep snow in the forest. There do not seem to be any hares around. The free forest workers have found a bear's den and are waiting for the snow to deepen before attacking it so that the bear cannot make a run for it.

The days should be getting longer, and yet it is still dark. Without the lights it is only possible to read between the hours of 9.30 a.m. and 3.30 p.m. = 6 hours. The rest of the time it is gloaming and night. Work begins at 8.00 a.m. and ends in the dark at 5.00 p.m., by which time the path back to our barracks is barely visible.

I found out from Irusya's letter that you cooked her pancakes when she was ill and told her about your visit to the cinema (it must have been 'Musical Story' you told her about). This made quite an impression upon me because though one ought to fall ill only rarely, and it should not therefore be the norm, when it does happen the relationship between a brother and sister is at its very best. It would be pointless to preach about this if the incident had not occurred, but since it did, and proved mutually beneficial, it is worth considering for a moment. It follows that to wish for such circumstances to repeat themselves is nothing more than a wish for something that you desire yourself. All that remains is to remember this positive experience and to develop an eagerness to continue treating your sister this way, for achieving this will be just as interesting as winning any other battle. This is what happiness is. You will find this to be the case throughout life.

The radio has been moved to a different place in the barracks. At the moment, the speakers are on a shelf hanging from the ceiling above the table; a mere five paces from my bed. It has quite an elegant design and I have been able to hear the broadcasts. It is turned on in our half of the barracks (can you see the switch on the bottom of one side?) in the morning at about 7.00 for the morning news broadcast. As soon as it is turned on I start getting up – the others lie in bed for another 20 minutes or so, until exercise, which, alas, nobody does (unlike in prison).

There are ashtrays and slop bowls on the table – all made from the tins and jars you sent. There is an inkwell too, and chess games are played every evening, with people gathered round to watch and support. [. . .]

Loudspeaker in the barracks, 22 December 1940.

Our camp is growing ever bigger – another barracks is being hastily built for invalids who are soon to arrive. (22.12.1940)

In extracts from letters to his wife Yablokov writes:

I could write a lot about the living conditions here, but I do not want to. Being surrounded by criminals is the hardest part; there are numerous thieves to contend with, in addition to lots of swearing, a lack of privacy, inconsiderate behaviour and an absence of both physical and moral hygiene . . .

This is the hardest aspect of our punishment – not the physical labour, nor the material conditions, but this . . . These people are the primary yoke of our oppression, with their thieving, abusive language and bad manners. What is more, the camp authorities treat them better than the 'politicals'.

The work itself is beyond my strength. We lift wet, very heavy railway sleepers, sometimes only lifting them in pairs. It is difficult to say whether I will manage to move to another type of work. It is not out of the question, but the choice of work here is extremely limited; there are no workshops, and political prisoners are never accepted into any work streams other than those carrying out general labour [. . .]. I will tell you about the food. Today's meals: at 5 a.m. – breakfast: 1st course – fish soup (although almost without fish); 2nd course – lentils. 'Lunch' (or dinner) is at 5.30 p.m. and consists of the same old cabbage soup, lentils and pasta . . .

Every day, as soon as morning light breaks . . . we head out to work in the forest. Most of the prison labourers work in 'wood felling' . . . but two of the work brigades, including my own, are allocated to 'stripping bark from sleepers'. This involves using a drawknife to remove the bark from wooden sleepers. It is not difficult, but the sleepers are heavy and lifting them onto the sawhorse and taking them away to the woodpile is especially hard . . . all this is done next to a railway track, which runs through the forest . . . We also walk along these tracks to get to work. The forest is damp and we leave in the

long shadows of evening, arriving at the barracks when
it is completely dark. We arrive and go to the canteen
where we receive our plate of stodgy oat soup, and then
spend the hours between 5.30 p.m. and 5.30 a.m. in the
barracks. We settle into the barracks, and by nightfall it
is warm enough, once the stove has been stoked. I have
been quite lucky with the position of my crib – it is
near the stove and away from the window. Bedbugs and
rats . . .

I will not complain. Somehow I will live on, even though
I am hungry and my strength is fading . . . Oh, how we
appreciate black bread!

In the summer of 1939 Yevgeny Yablokov's living conditions
improved a little. At first, he was allocated to a work brigade
tasked with finding and picking berries (preferable to the harder
labour of wood felling). Later, in mid-November, he was
sent to work in the 'technological-engineering' barracks as a
statistician. There he found himself among western-Ukrainian
political prisoners, and he wrote home: 'Everyone is getting on
in years [. . .] What joy – there is no more abusive language!'
He took part in camp amateur productions and even tried to
do some scientific research, growing a few rice seedlings on his
windowsill. He simply could not understand why a qualified
botanical specialist such as himself should not be allowed to
put his professional knowledge to use while imprisoned. 'Even
while I am isolated and temporarily distrusted politically, I could
still carry out my humble work in my specialised field in some
distant place. I could be put to great use, and trusted to work
utterly conscientiously', he wrote.

By January 1941, ill health had rendered even the most basic
physical work beyond him and Yablokov was reassigned to
the camp medical unit, where he carried out menial tasks as

a laboratory assistant. Before long, even this work proved too much for him. What was more, the prisoners' living conditions had significantly deteriorated during the war. Hunger was perpetual, and hopes of living to see their loved ones again faded with each passing day. Lines of thoughtful musings about man's destiny and fate began to appear more and more often in Yablokov's letters. 'I have begun to believe in fate,' he wrote. 'I believe that I will not return home until I have changed as a person, until I become cleverer, kinder and more strong-willed.'

At first, he had written almost daily, but as time went on, he was only permitted to write three letters per month, and then the number was reduced again, to just one. By 1943 he was only allowed to send one letter every three months. The letters were intercepted, 'lost', and some lines were erased by censorship. Nevertheless, Yablokov managed to get some of his letters and postcards to the post office via the free labourers, thereby bypassing camp administration, which goes a long way to explain their candid nature. One of his letters from 1943 contains the following sentence, 'Once again we have been restricted to sending one letter per month, but there are kind, and even very good people here . . .'

In 1943 Yevgeny Yablokov became entirely incapacitated for work. He was classified as an invalid and the order was given to resettle him in exile. While awaiting transportation, he continued to write home to Ryazan. His family read and reread his long (often several pages) letters aloud and discussed them. At the very outset of his ordeals, Yablokov had sent his wife the following prophetic lines: 'I was very touched by Irinochka's words that Yuri passed on in his letter to me: "It is a shame that Father's letters have stopped."'

Their father's letters stopped in March 1944.

Yuri Yevgenevich Yablokov graduated from the Hydrological Department of the Geographical Faculty of the Lomonosov

Moscow State University and served in the army during the Second World War. He was the chief hydrologist involved in the attempted reversal of the water flow of Siberian rivers in Central Asia. He worked on projects at several hydrological institutes and was employed by the Soviet Union's hydro-meteorology services. He also took part in the development of hydrological projects around the city of Mirny, in the Sayan Mountains, in addition to projects in Cuba and Cyprus.

Yablokov's daughter Irina (1923–2014) became an electrochemist and a space technology expert in a scientific research institute.

Victor Lunyov

'From Father — a letter to Alyona about a plucky postman . . .'

Victor Lunyov was born into a family of revolutionaries in 1909. His parents, Elena Mittelshtein and Yevgeny Lunyov, had met and married in exile in Russia's Vologda region in 1907. The family spent the year of the 1917 Revolution in Petrograd* before moving to Odessa on account of Yevgeny's ill health. Following his death from tuberculosis in 1920, Elena and her eleven-year-old son moved to Moscow, where she found work in an orphanage for abandoned children. The young Victor therefore spent the remainder of his childhood in the companionship of these orphans. In his autobiography, written in 1960, he says:

Victor Lunyov, Moscow, 1930s.

> I attended secondary school between 1923 and 1926, and then went on to study at the Plekhanov Institute of National Economy until 1930. I completed my third year at the Plekhanov Institute before the reorganisation of the

---

* Today St Petersburg.

institute resulted in my being transferred to the Moscow Higher Technical School, from where I also graduated in 1930. In December of that year I enrolled as a Postgraduate on a Masters programme at the Moscow Institute of Non-Ferrous Metals and Gold. I never completed this degree, as I was dispatched instead on a business assignment to the Sevkavtsink Factory, which was in need of a manager to run its distillation workshop. In 1934 I returned to Moscow, having been appointed head engineer at the Ministry of Non-Ferrous Metals. I wrote a book called 'Methods of Processing and Disposing of Zinc Ore', which was published in 1935 and later that year I was appointed director of construction at a metal plant in Chelyabinsk. I subsequently became the chief operator of the Karabash copper-smelting factory.

At first glance, Lunyov's autobiography appears to be a promising account of a young Soviet engineer with a keen interest in science, intent on playing an active role in the industrialisation of his country. By the time he enrolled at the Plekhanov Institute in 1927, Victor Lunyov had married Alexandra Leonidovna Paducheva, a former school friend (both had attended the prestigious School Number 5, where many notable people were educated) and by 1935 their daughter, Elena (affectionately known as Alyona), had been born. However, all was not quite as it seemed, for the NKVD had already been keeping a close eye on the young engineer for some time. In fact, Lunyov had first come to the attention of the watchful secret police in 1927, when he and some of his school friends had taken a shine to Trotskyism. They had read prohibited literature and criticised the general party line, but at that time his punishment was merely expulsion from the Komsomol. In order to 'atone for his sins' and 'prove himself trustworthy', the seventeen-year-old dissident went to work in a factory. He spent two years carrying out active community work, as a direct result of which he was not only reinstated into the Komsomol, but also received a recommendation to become a member of the All-Union Communist Party (the Bolsheviks).

Nevertheless, the damage had been done; he had been branded a Trotskyist and this episode in his life would come back to haunt him in February 1935, when he took on a role at the Karabash copper-smelting factory. Shortly after accepting the position of chief operator, the young engineer was summoned to explain and excuse the mistakes that he had made as a young member of the opposition at a meeting of the factory's Party activists. A two-page note that he wrote for his address at this meeting, in which he sought to assure those present of his loyalty to the Bolshevik Party, has survived:

> . . . My involvement – expulsion from KSM* for sharing certain ideas (uncertainty about the right side) vigilance . . . an interest in romanticism – influenced. Dissociated myself in good time.
> . . . Moscow School No.5, 1923–1925 political fights at school. Bolsheviks, Mensheviks, Socialist-Revolutionaries. From operating underground – to becoming leaders. Arrest of Mensheviks. Romanticism. Political upbringing. The Lessons of October[†] and The History of the AUCP[‡] by Zinovyev.[§]
> . . . Illegal Trotskyist literature: 1) secret party documents. 2) bulletins – current events. 3) Komsomol platform. Read

---

* Komsomol.

† 'The Lessons of October' is an article written by Leon Trotsky (1924) that was a hot topic of discussion in Party circles.

‡ All-Union Communist Party: Bolsheviks.

§ Grigory Zinovyev was a Bolshevik revolutionary and one of the seven members of the politburo, established in 1917.

Milman.* Results of 'being influenced' (hesitations about the right side).

. . . Building Socialism in one country – related to the question of a nation-state (childhood dreams). Didn't fully understand the peasant issue. Large quantity of polit. material – perhaps confused.

. . . Inter-party democracy. Trap for intelligentsia. Good lesson . . .(02.02.1935)

This time, however, his confession was of to avail. Victor Lunyov was arrested in September 1936 and charged with 'Trotskyism'. He was sentenced to ten years' imprisonment and sent to the Norillag labour camp in Siberia, where the NKVD ran an industrial complex: the Norilsk Plant. There was a growing need for expert engineers in the Arctic Circle at this time, and Victor Lunyov was put to work at the industrial plant.

The writer Sergey Snegov, a fellow prisoner of the Norillag, dedicated several pages of his memoirs to Lunyov. He remembers him as a striking and remarkable man. In his memoirs[†] he writes:

> It transpired that Victor possessed two particularly delightful qualities. Not only was he blessed with a clear, resonant and well-defined baritone, but he also knew a huge number of old Russian Romance[‡] and contemporary songs by heart. He once said of himself with a note of irony, 'My memory

---

* Gdaly Markovich Milman (1907–38) was a former student of Moscow's School No. 5, and a history teacher who worked with archives. From 1928 onwards he was subjected to political repression no less than five times. He was exiled and served sentences in several political detention centres and corrective labour camps. In 1938, while imprisoned at the Ukhta-Pechora Gulag (in the Komi Republic), he was sentenced to death and shot.

† Sergei Snegov, *The Tongue that Hates* (Moscow: Prosvet), 1991.

‡ Russian Romance is a genre of sentimental art song generally characterised by soulful melodies, lyricism and intensity.

is packed to the gunwales with Romance songs . . .!'

One day he proposed the following idea to me: 'You Sergei,' he said, 'know quite a few poems by heart. Let's have a competition to see who can remember the most. How about you recite poems, and I'll sing Romance?'

And so our evening concert commenced . . . Victor and I began with Pushkin's verses and Romance songs based upon Pushkin's poems. Before long, I realised, to my dismay, that I would lose the competition, for Victor knew more Romances than I knew poems. And when he sang four songs by four different composers based on my one poem, I became indignant.

'That's not fair, Victor. We did not agree that you would sing different Romances for the same one poem.'

He replied coolly, 'But neither did we agree that I could only sing one Romance for every poem. I must lay down a competitive margin. You will soon begin to destroy me with Pasternak and Mandelstam or Gumilyov and Kuzmin[*] and I know no Romances to go with their poems. Our argument continued for three evenings, and I managed to reach Tyutchev and Nekrasov[†] while Victor was still singing to Pushkin and Lermontov . . .'

Elena Victorovna Paducheva, Lunyov's daughter, said in an interview:

I remember my grandmother reminiscing about how Victor would sit and tell anecdotes. It was widely acknowledged that he was a joker and a jovial, vivacious man, and at home there would often be heated arguments about politics. Mother told me that at one point she had laid down an

---

[*] Prominent Russian and Soviet poets.
[†] Fyodor Tyutchev and Nikolai Nekrasov were nineteenth-century Russian poets.

ultimatum to my father, declaring, 'It's either me or Trotsky!' This was a phrase I remember well from my mother's stories. My parents' lives played out on a stormy set. One day my Mama tried to leave, but Father hid her shoes, so in a fit of fury she grabbed his watch and threw it out of the window. Fortunately, the watch landed on the window ledge and nothing was broken. They were both extremely quick-witted and spirited. Mother told me that they came up with an idea to pay one another twenty kopeks for each good one-liner. I do not believe that there was ever a shortage of witty and cutting exchanges in their lives.

By the time of his arrest, Victor Lunyov's marriage to Alexandra had broken down. Correspondence between husband and wife had ceased, and if there were any letters, none have survived. One item, however, was preserved – a wonderful handmade book, which Lunyov made in the camp for his little daughter Alyona. The book comprised a fairy tale in verse that Lunyov had composed about the North, and it was illustrated with beautiful drawings by an artist friend serving time in the camp alongside him. The artist went by the pseudonym GeFe, and his real name was only very recently discovered to be Georgiy Fyodorovich Baklanov (1894–1954). The poem and drawings were arranged into a short book, and the cover was artistically designed to resemble a postcard.

The illustrated booklet began with the following words: 'From Father – a letter to Alyona about a plucky postman . . .' and finished with a pencil-drawn portrait of the author, alongside the words:

Well, goodbye!
We will stop there.
I await your letters eagerly.
And send you a kiss, little daughter.

Here the fairy tale ends.
From me – your loving father.

Below are just a few examples of stanzas from Lunyov's fairy tale. The strict rhyme scheme has been forfeited in places so as to permit the most faithful reproduction of the thoughts and words of the author.

Book Cover
From: Father.
To: Letters to Alyona
About: A brave postman
From where: The Taymyr Peninsula/(don't be lazy – read it over and over again)

In December the blizzards howl
Darkness, wind, and falling snow.
It finds its way into nose and ears
Hurls, swirls and drifts . . .

. . . But when all around in quietness lies,
The wind is calm and the frost crackles,
The Nenets on sledges scud daringly by,
Steam rising from the reindeer's backs.

[. . .]

. . . Angry darkness, blizzards and cold
Try in vain to frighten those
Who are young at heart,
And clad in quilted trousers.

[. . .]

. . . There,
In front of the Kremlin towers
My family is gathered –
Granny
Little daughter
And Mama
Only I am missing.

There, where bridges without rivers sparkle
There, where gates stand without gates–
It is there that my dreams linger,
There, where Alyona waits.

[. . .]

The postman swiftly loads his sledge
And the reindeer break into a run . . .

. . . They reach the river with the letter
Eat their lunch beside a stove
Warm their hands and feet a little
And continue on along the road.

. . . Along the winding Siberian river
The postman carries the letter across the ice
By dog
By car
By reindeer
By rail.

[. . .]

House Number 16
Driver! Stop!

On the door the postman knocks
Does Alyona live here?
Her father has sent her a letter!

Victor Lunyov was imprisoned at the Norillag until February 1942, at which point, as he writes in his autobiography, 'The Military Collegium of the USSR Supreme Court decided to revoke my charge of Trotskyism'. Nevertheless, Lunyov remained in Norilsk until 1946, working of his own volition as a dispatcher at the industrial plant, and later as the head of the quality control department. Sometime prior to this, he had married his second wife, and was now father to another a little girl called Tanya. His first wife, and daughter Elena, remained in Moscow with his mother, Elena Lunyov-Mittelshtein.

Lunyov left Norilsk in 1946. Finding himself barred from Moscow and other large cities in the Soviet Union, he decided to relocate to eastern Kazakhstan. There he worked as the head of the manufacturing department at the Irtysh copper-smelting plant, and later as senior engineer in the scientific research department of the Leninogorsk plant.

But the ever-watchful secret police organs had not forgotten him. In 1950 he was arrested once again on the same charge as before: affiliation to Trotskyism. The Special Board of

MGB* sentenced him by default to another ten years in a labour camp.

Lunyov managed to visit his first wife and daughter twice during the years between his prison terms. In 1943 he travelled to Samarkand,† where his mother, former wife and daughter were then living, having been evacuated from Moscow following the outbreak of war. This visit is one of his daughter's most vivid childhood memories. She recalls:

> My father had bought me a doll from somewhere, like Jean Valjean for Cosette. It was a real doll, and I remember it as well as if I were holding it now. Until then, the other little girls and I had sewn our own dolls from scraps of cloth and old sheets, drawing on the faces ourselves. But this was a real doll; she looked practically alive! Against the backdrop of our lives at that time, she seemed to me to be something otherworldly.

Sometime later, Lunyov went to stay with them again, this time in Moscow, and this visit was also firmly imprinted in Elena's memory. She remembers that her father

> announced that my mother and grandmother deserved a break from housework. He took us to the restaurant 'Seventh Heaven' on the seventh floor of the Hotel Moskva. I had never been to a restaurant before this and it would be many years before I would visit one again. For us, dining out was something celebratory and very out of the ordinary.

---

* The MGB is the abbreviated name for the Ministry of State Security. This was the name given to the Soviet intelligence agency between the years of 1946 and 1953. Prior to this the MGB was the NKVD, and later it would become the KGB.

† A city in southeastern Uzbekistan.

Father and daughter then had their photograph taken together, and Elena carefully stowed the photo away in her family archive.

Victor Lunyov with his daughter, Elena. Moscow, 1948.

Elena said:

> I remember his second arrest very clearly. At that time, we lived on Gorokhovsky Lane. The apartment had initially been designed for one family but it had since been turned into a Kommunalka* and was shared by three families. We shared one room, right at the far end of one corridor. I remember hearing the doorbell ring. Mother was away at work or on a business trip, as usual, so I was with my grandmother. I walked down the long corridors and opened the door. It turned out to be a telegram from my father's daughter, Tanya, in Leninogorsk. It read, 'Papa has fallen ill again. Tanya'.
> 'Oh well . . .' I thought.
> I carried the telegram through to my grandmother, who clasped her head in her hands in sorrow. (Unlike Elena, her grandmother – a former revolutionary well versed in secrecy – understood the meaning of the words 'fallen ill

---

* A communal apartment shared by several families.

again' perfectly.) And that is how the news of my father's second arrest reached us. I was by then fifteen years old, and I remember taking the suburban train to Pushkino station (on the Yaroslavl line) in order to send a parcel – they would not take it in Moscow. My grandmother had gathered some things into a wooden box and she taught me how to tie it up correctly with string before I took it to the post office.

Victor Lunyov was finally released in 1954. He was rehabilitated in 1957 and managed to publish two short volumes: *Words on Lead* (Moscow: Metallurgy, 1964) and *Get to Know Copper* (Moscow: Metallurgy, 1965). However, Sergei Snegov describes his former campmate's freedom as an 'unhappy' one; he lived with a devastating lung disease. Lunyov died in 1964 at the age of fifty-four.

Elena went on:

> I saw my father for the final two times when he came to Moscow to undergo medical treatment for his cancer. On the first occasion, in the very early 60s, he ran away from hospital and arrived at my mother's birthday party in his hospital pyjamas! The second time, I was with him in hospital; it was not long before his death. I remember him saying to me, 'Here I am, lying on this bed, and the man in the bed next to me is a KGB man. You could say that he is my prison guard. And yet we both share the same fate.' This was the last time that I saw my father.

Elena, Victor Lunyov's eldest daughter, graduated from the Faculty of Philology at the Lomonosov Moscow State University. She was a talented linguist, and worked as a senior scientist at the All-Russian Institute for Scientific and Technical Information. She became a Doctor of Philological Sciences and a member of the American Academy of Arts and Sciences. Elena authored six studies and several hundred publications in Russian, English, French and Polish.

Tatiana (Tanya) Lunyova (1933–2012), Victor Lunyov's daughter from his second marriage, graduated from the Biology Faculty at Tomsk University and studied for her postgraduate degree under her stepsister's tutelage. She lived in Ust-Kamenogorsk, Kazakhstan.

Mikhail Lebedev

'Papa, can you hear me?'

The line above is from the memoirs of Yanina Lebedeva. Her memoirs are stored in Memorial's archives, alongside letters from her father, Mikhail Lebedev, who wrote home from Zlatoust Prison and the Kolyma Gulag between 1938 and 1946.

Mikhail Lebedev's life unfolded in much the same way as that of many of his contemporaries. He was born in 1892 into a family of railway mechanics in the city of

Mikhail Lebedev, 1934

Suwałki* in the Grodno† Governorate of what was then the Russian Empire. He finished school before the Revolution, earning a little money on the side by tutoring alongside his studies and in 1918, having married and graduated as a qualified doctor from the Medical Faculty at Kiev University, he took a job as a medical assistant to a privately practising doctor in Kiev. His daughter, Yanina, was born in 1920. From 1919 until his demobilisation in 1929, he served as a doctor in the Red

---

* Today this is a city in Poland.
† Today this is a city in Belarus.

Army, before moving to Ivanovo to work in the Public Health Administration until 1933. He was subsequently put in charge of the city health department of Kostroma, and by the time he was arrested in 1937, he had been appointed chief physician at the Neurological-Therapeutic Hospital in Yaroslavl.

In her memoirs Yanina Lebedeva recalls:

> Saying goodbye to my father on the night of 22 to 23 September 1937 has remained etched so clearly in my memory it is as though it were yesterday. That night, I didn't feel like sleeping. I had just started at the Teaching Institute, and was adjusting to a new, unfamiliar and initially challenging life. I had always been a light sleeper and found it difficult to fall asleep. My mother and father had been on their guard since my father had been called to a gorkom* city council cabinet meeting on 11 September and subsequently expelled from the Party.
>
> We were then living in a room at the Yaroslavl Neurological-Therapeutic Hospital, where my father was chief physician, because it had been difficult to get an apartment of our own in Yaroslavl. At half past one in the morning there came a knock on the door. My mother and father got up quickly. I awoke too (my bed was behind the large wardrobe) and immediately heard unfamiliar voices. I got dressed. They began the search. We were all silent; they had forbidden us to speak, even quietly. In any case, we didn't feel like talking in front of such people – their very presence was so loathsome. One of the NKVD men even took my father to the lavatory. My mother and I hurriedly gathered a few permitted items. Once my father had left the room, my mother began to cry. She cried quietly, so quietly. (Until this point I had almost never seen her cry; she was

* The gorkom was the City Committee of the All-Union Communist Party (Bolsheviks).

very strong-willed, as was my father.) Mama stayed in the room, and I left to accompany my father out to the staircase. I walked in a stupefied daze along the familiar hospital corridors, through the vestibule and out onto the staircase. It was early morning; the sun was just beginning to rise. Such a beautiful, bright September morning was breaking. My father was dressed in a dark greenish coat and a dark blue peaked hat, which he wore in Lenin's style. His face was weary and unshaven. They hurried him down the steps. I followed, unable to stop myself. When he reached the bottom of the steps, my father turned his head. 'It's a shame that I couldn't set you on your feet,' he said. I couldn't answer. They hurried him out. I stood at the foot of the stairs. In front of me rose a line of dark green trees, illuminated in the morning sun, and three figures walked along the road . . . they turned a corner, and then disappeared. I cannot put it into words, but I can still see my father's face now, with all of its lines and wrinkles . . . That is how we parted.

Mikhail Lebedev was convicted of participation in a counter-revolutionary organisation affiliated to Trotsky and Bukharin* and sentenced to ten years' imprisonment. He was initially sent to a prison in the city of Zlatoust in the southern Urals, before being moved to a labour camp at Kolyma. While at Kolyma he wrote a letter of 'complaint' to the Prosecutor's Office of the USSR containing the following lines:

The investigators of the Yaroslavl NKVD employed
physical methods of persuasion that amounted to torture

---

* Translator's note: Nikolai Bukharin was a Bolshevik revolutionary and a former high-ranking party member prior to his expulsion from the Politburo in 1929. Having clashed with Stalin while in government, he was arrested in 1937 and executed in 1938 following a show trial during which he was accused of engaging in counter-revolutionary activities aimed at overthrowing the party leadership.

during the investigation. The first interrogation, for
instance, lasted for six uninterrupted days and nights,
during which I was denied a single minute of sleep. I was
also denied permission to get up from my chair at any
point. During the following interrogations I was held for
three to four days without intervals. The interrogators
changed shifts, yet I was required to remain seated
throughout . . . However, none of their 'methods' could
extort from me a confession of something that I never
did . . .

In letters to his wife and daughter, Felya and Yanusya as
he affectionately called them, Mikhail Lebedev wrote almost
nothing about his suffering. There is only one letter from
Zlatoust in which he touched upon his life in prison, but he
only mentioned it because at this point he still firmly believed
that he was soon to be released. It was written to his seventeen-
year-old daughter:

You ask whether I am working. No, Yanusenka; I am
serving a sentence. I am in prison, not in a labour camp.
Receiving parcels is forbidden (except for money). I do
not need a coat, hat or underpants – we wear standard
issue prison clothes. My trousers are really quite worn out,
but I have no use for them, except for returning home
when I am released. And they will do for that purpose. It
would be good if you did not have to sell anything, but if
you must, then sell my winter jacket and keep my trousers
and boots, as without them I will have nothing to wear
when I am out. I am using my glasses, which I brought
with me – I can no longer read without them. They are
serving me well at the moment, but when the time comes
to replace them, I will have to buy new ones here as it
is forbidden to have them sent. My books were lost in

Yaroslavl so I am reading a fictional novel and learning German. I have made marked progress. Reading and studying German helps pass the time and keeps me from feeling melancholy . . . (06.10.1938)

There are no other references to his life as a prisoner. His letters served one purpose alone – providing moral support to his loved ones by bolstering them and instilling a sense of hope. Below are several extracts from his letters:

Dear Yanusya,
It does not make me happy to hear that Mama reads my letters every morning and evening. I would feel better if I knew that she left them alone and was lively, or even laughed! Picking at and reopening your wounds may well seem preferable to leaving them be and distracting yourself from them, but it is not helpful. I cannot reproach you for hanging your head and losing heart. But it is time, already high time, to buck up! You absolutely must pull yourselves together. [. . .] You need to get a hold of yourself and muster all of your energy, all of your strength. In my dreams and in my waking hours I picture what it will be like when I return to you; how we will greet each other, kiss each other, and all be together! [. . .] You must comfort yourselves with this thought and wait for my return. And when you feel better; once you learn to smile once again, my life within these four walls will become easier too. (27.07.1938)

Dear Yanusya and Felya!
Surely you can understand that it tortures me to see how you have wilted and hang your heads and hands? How is it that you cannot see that when you are cheerful, upbeat and fighting life with tenacity, with good cheer and

Photo of Yanina Lebedeva sent to her father
in prison, 1938.

gusto ('life, you won't get the better of us'), it will be easier for me than when your 'mood is terrible and you are utterly apathetic'. [. . .] I received and am now looking at Yanusya's photograph, but the girl that I left behind is no longer anywhere to be seen. Instead, a grown–up woman looks back at me; pensive, with a serious face tinged with sadness. Yet those features are so dear and familiar. Oh, how I wish that I could be with you so that face could light up with joy. Do not lose heart. We shall wait. (11.08.1938)

I simply cannot think what advice to give you. My inability to help weighs heavily upon me, and yet I see that you need help to get through this suffering. [. . .] No, I cannot begin to express how much this awareness of my powerlessness to help you troubles me [. . .] But even though I cannot help you in any practical sense, let me at least warm you a little with words of love; my love for you which knows no limits, which you must feel through all the walls and across the kilometres. And hope. You must believe that life will not always be so unjustly cruel. And if it cannot be so for us old folk, then Yanusya at least must smile eventually, and her happiness will be our happiness too. Look after her, Felya! (26.10.1938)

Felya, my darling sweetheart; Yanusya, my dear,
I hear everything you say, I feel it all and worry terribly
about you. Your pain hurts me far more than my own.
If only I could . . . If it were up to me, I would carry a
load two or three times heavier, just to keep you from
this agony. To have my hands tied, and to be powerless
to help you, is harder for me than coping with my own
worries. It pains me that even my words and letters – the
only way that I am still able to help – are too weak, too
uninspiring to have an effect. And I so desperately want to
instil in you the energy, and strength, and hope, and faith,
of which you are so in need. (01.03.1939)

Life without a father and husband was extremely hard for
the Lebedev family. Yanina was forced to leave the teaching
institute where she was studying. Nobody would employ either
mother or daughter, and there was nothing to live on; they were
starving. His daughter spoke openly about this in her letters to
her father, but he did not know how to help them. His advice
was heavy with despair.

A daughter is not responsible for her father, and yet your
punishment has proven to be worse than my own: soon
you will not even have rations or a roof over your head,
which I at least have in prison. No, this must not be! In
a Soviet country one should not die from hunger and
unemployment. It is absurd! This is what I suggest you
do: go to the local NKVD department and to the regional
procurator and explain your situation to them. [. . .] In
any case, there is no need to be rash and no need to lose
hope until the very last minute. And don't you dare hide
anything from me. Your omissions do not serve their
purpose; rather, they frighten me even more. (26.09.1938)

In her memoirs Yanina Lebedeva writes:

> Rereading my father's letters, I have to say that he sometimes unfairly accused my mother of crying and of being faint-hearted. This was absolutely not the case. I have always had a deep respect for my mother and am extremely grateful for the immense courage, tenacity and energy that she displayed in the circumstances in which we found ourselves, which were especially difficult for the first few months. I was not like her: I was lost, frightened, despondent and apathetic. But Mama bore her cross resolutely and always sought to raise my spirits and instil in me belief in a better future. She really was a mother, father and best friend to me.

A letter from Mikhail Lebedev says:

> Yanusya! Your task is to use this time as preparation for life. Pay less attention to the wounds that life has inflicted upon you, and focus on working on yourself. I am an old man, yet I continue to study doggedly, even though I have doubts as to how useful this information will be to me in the circumstances. But you are young! You should be ashamed of yourself. I am expecting to hear the following news from you: What is your library like? What are you reading? Would you like to take me on in a little German competition? Although, it might be better for you to think of attending an extramural teaching institute. (26.01.1939)

Did Mikhail Lebedev really believe that he would be freed? Either way, he continued to wait, and to hope. There is no question that he was ever a member of the opposition and we can believe without a shadow of a doubt his statement made in the aforementioned 'complaint' to the USSR Procurator's office: 'I have never committed a single crime against the Soviet state. I am the son of a labourer; a railway mechanic, and I owe all of my knowledge, my labours of love and everything that I have achieved in life, to the Soviet state.'

Below are extracts from letters that he wrote to his family:

> When we are reunited again we will sort everything
> out and set things to rights. Roll on our reunion. It is
> currently the second anniversary celebration of the Great
> October Revolution but we are celebrating apart, and
> in such sorrow. However, on this special occasion in
> particular; on the day when we celebrate the liberation
> of the oppressed, I believe particularly ardently that if not
> now, then very soon, we too will feel the same heady
> joy and good cheer as did all those who dedicated their
> lives so earnestly to the emancipation of the workers.
> (01.11.1938)

> Sweet, dear Yanusya and Felya,
> Surely you have received a letter from me by now?
> This is the fourth month, for goodness sake. [. . .] Your
> despondency saddens me greatly. You simply must pull
> yourselves together. It goes without saying that with the
> attitude displayed in your letters you can expect nothing
> but more misfortune. Life favours those who can maintain
> their composure. When you are in a constant state of
> sadness and apathy, all of life's luck will slip through your
> fingers. If you love each other, and me, then you must
> not seek to spoil each other's moods. Instead you should
> be raising each other's spirits. It is a real shame if you
> never received my letter in which I wrote about this in a
> little more detail. [. . .] I will use this opportunity to send
> you both a great many kisses . . . and to tell you to stop
> moping! You are two single, interesting young women.

Who is there for whom to fight for happiness and good
fortune, if not for you two? You are lucky – you have
each other, and two heads are better than one. Yes . . .
you were smart and spirited when there was no need
to be so, and now that such conduct is required of you,
why, suddenly you are behaving like wet chickens . . . Oh
dear, oh dear, what a shame! Why do I still love you so?
I do love you for some reason, but it has been dampened;
gone limp and blurry. I can't pinpoint it again until it
dries out . . . What is more, nobody else will be able to
see it either. 'She's a depressing girl,' they'll think. 'Don't
go too close or you'll be infected by her dreariness for a
week!' Who can shake you out of this, once and for all?
Oh, Yanusya, my darling daughter. I must say, you do
take after your mother. Oh, that Mama of yours! Anyway,
I am sending you another kiss. M. Lebedev (22.02.1939)

In June 1939, Lebedev was transported from Zlatoust to
Kolyma. In his letters from the camp, just as in his previous
letters from the prison, he almost never mentioned his own
experiences and suffering. He very briefly and sparingly alluded
to the fact that general labourers at Kolyma worked in the mines,
but he never mentioned the hunger and sickness. Neither did he
reveal that he had fallen seriously ill, and had consequently been
reassigned to work as an assistant to the camp doctor. In truth,
he had begun to notice some irregularities in his correspondence
with his family, who had by then moved to Ufa. Letters that
had once come and gone regularly were becoming increasingly
sporadic, so he began to send telegrams instead, congratulating
Yanina on her birthday and on her graduation from the medical
institute in Ufa where she had resumed her studies. He began
to suspect that letters from the camp deemed to be containing
'undesirable' information were not being sent. It was a concern
that he had voiced in previous letters from Zlatoust:

Now a word about me. I am in good health and as chipper as ever, especially since you have sorted things out. Learning German is still my main occupation and really I have nothing new to add as everything is just the same as it was before. What changes could there possibly be? Life goes on monotonously from day to day, in the same routine. I tried to describe this routine in a letter to you, but the letter did not arrive, which means there is no need to write about such things. I could write about my hopes? But there is no point in reopening our old wounds . . . (12.01.1939)

Lebedev's health deteriorated significantly and as a result of the severity of his illness, the camp authorities reduced his sentence by eighteen months. He was discharged from the Kolyma Gulag on 21 March 1946, having been deprived of his civil rights for a further five years.

Yanina's memoirs contain the following poignant lines about her reunion with her father:

Mikhail Lebedev after his release in the village of Mikoyanovka (Belgorod Region), 1946.

My father came home in June 1946. He had been released early, in March of that year, having been deemed 'unfit to work' due to his health – he was suffering from stomach cancer. He had been diagnosed with cancer in 1945, but the doctors had assured him that they had 'invented' this illness so as to classify him as unfit to work and thus enable him to return home early. This is what my father told us when he returned the following year. At that time, I was managing the regional hospital, where I had been working since 1943. We were living in a tiny room in the hospital, into which we had just about been able to squeeze two beds and a table. [. . .] At dawn, a little after four o'clock in the morning (this is when the work train arrived from Kursk), somebody knocked at the door (the hospital was only two hundred metres from the station). I automatically jumped out of bed, threw on my dress and went to open the door. I quickly flung it open. Outside it was already completely light. I had so wanted to stay in bed . . . An elderly man with a yellowish face like a Chinese man and lively black eyes stood before me. He had a grey moustache and was thin and stooping. He wore a quilted khaki-coloured jacket and a peaked cap of the same shade, dark riding breeches and canvas knee-high boots.

I stood looking at him, half-awake and rather disgruntled, thinking gloomily, 'He's probably going to call me out to deliver a child somewhere.' The man was silent and stared at me intently. The eyes looked slightly quizzically and irritatingly happily at me. I waited for him to say something. He was silent. Neither of us said anything for quite a long time. I started to feel annoyed – he had woken me up, and was now standing there saying nothing. What did he want? And yet at the same time I saw something good in his face and I couldn't bring myself to demand anything. Finally I could bear it no longer. 'What do you want?' I asked. And suddenly, such a familiar, dear voice asked quietly, 'Don't you recognise me?' That voice, that voice! I knew it immediately. I was completely taken aback and began to tremble. Then I ran down the stairs to him and we both began to cry. [. . .] How he got there, I do not know. He was very sick, with a broken rib and a body exhausted from dystrophy. He had arrived on the work train from Kursk, having changed trains along the way, and carried with him his paltry possessions: an old quilt, a change of underwear, boots, some small bits and bobs, and a half-litre jar of red caviar that he had brought all the way from Kolyma. Despite his desperate hunger along the journey, he had carried this jar of caviar with him and, reaching for it with trembling hands, he said, 'This is for Mama. She always so loved red caviar and it is difficult to get hold of these days.' [. . .]

Even at home he could not relax. We were tortured by poverty, malnutrition and the cold. It was bitterly cold in the apartment and my father would feel the cold terribly. He sat in his woollen boots, his cheap old trousers and prison-issue quilted jacket, hiding his cold, thin hands in his sleeves and huddled up against the chill. 'When I was at Kolyma, I never imagined for a moment that you were living like this,' he said. 'Perhaps I should not have come. It would have been better to have stayed there – life here is hard enough for you as it is without having me here, ill. Had I stayed, you would have believed me dead and resigned yourselves to that thought.' It was frightening to hear this, but what could we do?

Mikhail Lebedev died in 1949 and was fully rehabilitated posthumously in 1957. His wife outlived him by nine years. Yanina recalls that her mother 'treasured my father's letters, always rereading them and drawing strength from them'.

She especially loved the letter in which my father recalled the time that she had spent at the front with him, enduring all the challenges of the military campaign – at first pregnant, and later with a three-month old daughter. She also remembered the lines in which he wrote that she was now 'both mother and father to me'. In truth, I could always turn to either my mother or my father and say, in

Gogol's words, 'Papa, can you hear me?' My courageous and admirable parents would always hear my call.

Unfortunately we have no further information about Yanina Lebedeva's life. She gave the letters from her father and her memoirs to Memorial in 1989, at which time she lived in Okhtyrka, in the Sumy region of Ukraine.

Ivan Sukhanov

'I think about you all the time'

Ivan Sukhanov was born in 1881 in the village of Novodevichy on the Volga River. The village was a fairly large commercial hub, with a church that rose high into the sky on the banks of the river. Sukhanov's great-grandfather, born into serfdom, had run the village watermill. The Sukhanovs clung resolutely to a legend identifying the origins of their family name. The story is that a group of Tatar grain merchants had appeared at the

Ivan Sukhanov, Riga, 1910.

watermill one day and addressed Ivan's great-grandfather with the words 'Su-khan', which in Tatar means 'Ruler of Water'. Thus the surname 'Sukhanov' was born. Ivan Sukhanov's father owned a small business himself and worked as the representative of a Russo-Belgian company trading in eggs. He purchased eggs and sent them to St Petersburg to be sold.

Ivan Sukhanov, the only son in a family of six, attended the parish school in Novodevichy and went on to receive his secondary education at the Realschule in Samara. Although he left before completing all nine years of his education, it was there in Samara that his talents for mathematics, art and music (he played the violin) really came to the fore.

After much painful contemplation and numerous arguments with his father, who wanted him to take on the family business, Sukhanov earned a place at the Riga Polytechnical Institute. He graduated in 1910 with a degree in architectural engineering and moved to the St Petersburg Academy of Arts, where he continued his architectural studies, taking a course under the tutelage of the prominent Russian artist Alexandre Benois. While studying, Sukhanov worked as a tutor and sold his own paintings to support himself; his father had refused to give him any financial assistance. He continued to pursue his passion for music and took private violin lessons alongside his academic courses. Blessed with a wonderful ear for music, he played many different instruments and was even offered a place in the Riga Symphony Orchestra. He turned this down, however, choosing instead to focus his attentions on architecture and painting.

While in St Petersburg, Sukhanov met a young woman called

Ivan Sukhanov (holding guitar), Novodevichy, 1908.

Sofia Obrezova, who was studying on the Bestuzhev Courses.[*] She had been born into a family of Cossacks in the city of Vladikavkaz and her father was a major general and head of the Caucasus Military District. Sofia shared Ivan's passion for music and loved Russian Silver Age poetry, theatre and painting. The two were married in 1916 and the first of four children, a son called Mikhail (Misha), was born in 1917.

Sofia and Ivan Sukhanov with their son, Misha. Ulyanovsk, 1918.

In 1916, Sukhanov was summoned to work as an architect at a munitions factory in the city of Simbirsk.[†] The project was completed in 1920, but the couple stayed on in Simbirsk, where Sukhanov had been given a teaching job at the Middle-Volga Region Architectural Training College. During these years he also found the time to teach history of art and produce paintings and drawings of his own for exhibitions. By 1924, Ivan Sukhanov had become the regional chief engineer for the Ulyanovsk Governorate.

---

[*] Founded in 1878, the Bestuzhev Courses in St Petersburg were Imperial Russia's largest and most prominent establishment for women's education.
[†] Today Ulyanovsk.

The family moved to Moscow in 1929 and settled in the country suburb of Malakhovka. They bought a plot of land, built a house and planted a small garden. Ivan fell in love with Malakhovka, with the little Pekhorka River and its lake. During those happy years he painted an entire collection of landscape portraits, the pictures radiating the light, peace and joy that emanated from the Malakhovka countryside.

His young son, Misha, also took up drawing and Sukhanov tutored him, helping him to master the art of perspective, composition, and a variety of different drawing techniques. It was the happiest period of Sukhanov's life: he was a highly successful architect teaching and working on all sorts of interesting projects with a number of different organisations. His most significant architectural projects were largely public buildings: theatres in the Sormovsky district and in Samarkand, a school in Orsk, an outpatient clinic in Vyksa, a bank in Syktyvkar and the Narkomles* building in Moscow. In the spirit of the time, he also designed a memorial project for the revolutionary fighters of Ulyanovsk and Kolomna. He was nominated for prizes in All-Union competitions for many of his works, and several of his projects won awards. His plans for standard school and residential buildings, hospitals and village reading rooms were among those published by the Ulyanovsk Provincial Planning Committee and the Gubispolkom.†

This calm and peaceful life came to an abrupt end on 4 December 1934. Ivan Sukhanov was arrested early in the morning while his wife was at church and his sixteen-year-old son still lay asleep. The arrest came as a huge shock to him, for though he was loyal to the Soviet state, he was not a member of the All-Union Communist Party (Bolsheviks)‡, and his focus had

---

* People's Commissariat of the Timber Industry.
† Provincial Soviet Executive Committee.
‡ Translator's note: And therefore not at risk of falling victim to one of the purges of Party members.

been upon practising his beloved architecture. Perhaps, however, he had inadvertently allowed a few ambiguous comments to pass his lips when among his closest circle of friends.

Shortly after his arrest, he was charged with 'counter-revolutionary activity' in accordance with Article 58. He was held in both the Lubyanka and Butyrka prisons until a Special Board of NKVD sentenced him on 27 February 1935 to five years in a corrective labour camp. From 1935 to 1936, he served his sentence in the SibLag, in the town of Temirtau (Kazakhstan). There, he continued to carry out his former architectural work, designing residential houses and railway stations for small rail hubs (a new branch of the railway track was being built around Temirtau). All the while, camp letters and postcards steadily wended their way back towards his wife and son at Number 2, Shkolnaya Street in Malakhovka.

Every single letter mentions his son, Misha, whom Sukhanov dreamed of watching become an architect. He worried about Misha's final school grades and advised him on how best to prepare for the Architectural Institute's entrance exams:

> My sweet Mishka,
>
> I received your postcard. [. . .] I too suspected that your school in Malakhovka would not equip you with the necessary knowledge for the competitive entrance exams. Besides an understanding of the subject, you must also quickly make yourself familiar with the necessary skills. You must develop proficiency in both mathematics and in drawing. All this will come if you study diligently, and I would be very pleased if you got out Shmulevich's textbook and worked through all of the exercises. Write to me and let me know whether you decide to attend a preparatory course or to continue working with Sergei Ivanovich in his studio. In terms of receiving the best preparation for the exams, the course would of course be

best, but I am very concerned that it would be extremely
hard for your mother. Try to put your watercolour
paintings up for sale. I received your parcel and am very
grateful for it. Tomorrow we have a day off. I will write
you a proper letter. [. . .] I am sending you a kiss. Your
loving I. S. (11.09.1935)

. . . I am very interested in Misha's studies. How is he
getting on with his latest tests and when will he finish his
exam preparations? I expect that the entrance exams will
take place in June or July – presumably term will have
ended by May. Is there any way he can get in without
sitting examinations or must he sit them in every subject?
I think that he feels significantly better prepared than
he did last year and the results of his regular study speak
for themselves. Can Misha apply for a place in both the
architectural department and the painting department so
that if for some reason he does not get into the first, he
can nevertheless get a place in the second? I believe that
there is now an artistic training college in Moscow too?
A few days ago I read in 'Izvestiya' that the Academy
of Architecture has just published a book on Palladio's*
architecture. I would really like Misha to make sure he
buys it as soon as it is comes out on sale. If it contains
reproductions of Palladio's work, it will be a very useful
book . . . (08.05.1936)

In August 1936 Sukhanov began his *etap*† to the Dmitlag.
Once there, he worked in the project bureau for the construction

---

* In 1937 the All-Union Academy of Architecture's publishing house in
Moscow released the work of the celebrated sixteenth-century Italian architect
Andrei Palladio, *Four Books about Architecture*.

† Translator's note: The 'etap' was the long and tortuous train journey endured
by prisoners, often for weeks or months, when travelling to designated prison
camps.

Portraits of 'zeka' by I. Sukhanov, Dmitlag, 1936.

of the Moscow-Volga Canal. Prisoners who worked on the construction of this canal in the 1930s were known as the 'prisoner-canal army', which was later abbreviated to 'zeka'.* In every camp that he found himself – at Temirtau, the Dmitlag and later Chibyu – Sukhanov would draw pencil sketches of camp life and portraits of the prisoners whenever he had time to spare. He also worried constantly about Misha.

> My dear, sweet Misha! I did receive your postcard. I am
> very pleased to hear that you are going to exhibitions and
> showing an interest in other artists' work. In my opinion,
> your observation that your fellow Academy students'
> work lacks personality is spot-on. Indeed, therein lies the
> main weakness of their work.
>   [. . .] Art takes its truest form when the artist is true
> to himself. And a teacher who does not value his pupil's

---

* 'zeka' is an abbreviation of *zaklyuchenniye-kanaloarmeyitsi* meaning 'prisoner-canal army'. The word 'zek' has since become a commonly used colloquial word for 'prisoner'.

Barracks, Temirtau. 1935–36.

An aerial view of the barracks, Temirtau, 1935–1936.

individualism is a poor teacher, just as a pupil who does not develop his own individuality is a poor student. The pupil's task is to work on his drawing style, to draw with love and reverence and to be frank and diligent, working tirelessly on himself. And we must love nature, our greatest teacher, with all our soul, and guard ourselves against banality as we would protect ourselves from a

Aerial view of barracks, Temirtau. 1935–36.

Camp kitchen, Temirtau. 1935–36.

dangerous disease. Go to the Byalinitsky* exhibition. He has his own style and a few decent sketches. It is a shame that you cannot (and do not like to) draw at home, but nevertheless you absolutely must learn algebra and arithmetic. I think about you all the time, and hope that with determination and commitment you will achieve a great deal.

I am sending you a hug and a kiss. Your loving father. (07.04.1936)

. . . I have just received a postcard from Misha. I am very pleased to hear that he is excelling at drawing, but why is his watercolour painting not so good? He will only need to work with paint or indian ink, but in any case, sketching forms the basis of everything. I am trying to draw as much as possible and in my free time I draw portraits. I think I will soon start to draw with a quill and ink, and strongly advise Misha to draw with a quill too. It is very helpful, and architects in particular must be able to work with quills. I am currently designing tunnel entrances, one of which is already in use. I shall await a detailed letter from Misha with an account of how he got on in his exams in the other subjects. He can do a little painting outdoors from life over the summer, but for now let him concentrate on the sciences. (24.04.1936)

. . . I am so happy for Misha that his work is being exhibited and am very grieved to have been deprived of the opportunity to see his drawings in the museum. He must compare his drawings with those of others on display and draw from them some useful lessons. These exhibitions are very valuable. I like the fact that Misha decided to

---

★ The landscape artist V. K. Byalinitsky-Birulya (1872–1957) whose personal exhibition was held in Moscow in 1936.

work solely on his drawing this winter, provided that is, that you are able to make ends meet . . . (27.09.1937)

My darling, sweet Misha! I received your letter and it made me very happy. I am so pleased that you are beginning to assemble some architectural designs. If you have time, construct a model of a circular summerhouse – the structure is very interesting and it will be very picturesque against a backdrop of trees. You will need to draw the trees only as a backdrop, and very faintly, so that the architectural composition stands out more strongly. Have a look at my Kurbatov* book and read over both France and Italy in Parks and Gardens. I have sketched here [letter] a summerhouse with two bridges. The design that you sent was not bad either, but it would be harder to construct. I wish you success. Work as hard as you can and trace copies of good architecture on tissue paper. Buy the Palladio book and draw the ledges and profiles. In the summer you must go and make sketches from life of the architecture at Kuzminski, Arkhangelskoye and other interesting places in the vicinity. I am sending you and your mother a kiss. I look forward to you writing again and telling me how your project went. Your loving Ivan. (04.05.1938)

Before long, Ivan Sukhanov was transported from the Dmitlag to the Ukhtpechlag (specifically, the village of Chibyu in the Komi ASSR).† His son remembers that Sukhanov had wanted to remain at the Dmitlag, engineering canal-locks and coming up with different designs. This was the work that he knew and loved after all, and the regime at the Dmitlag was also slightly

---

* V. Y. Kurbatov's *Parks and Gardens: History and Theory of Landscape Design* (Petrograd, 1916).
† ASSR is an abbreviation of Autonomous Soviet Socialist Republic.

less restrictive than that of the more northerly Ukhtpechlag. However, his efforts to resist transfer proved futile.

Sukhanov was granted an early release in 1938 but having been 'deprived of his civil rights' and therefore barred from major cities such as Moscow, he was unable to return to his family in Malakhovka. He took up a post as an architect in a design firm in Syktyvkar until 1939, when he began working for the Moscow Academy of Architecture in Yegoryevsk. In August 1940 he settled in Vladimir and took a job at the regional history museum, overseeing the restoration of the Dmitrievsky Cathedral.

He was arrested again on 4 July 1941 'on suspicion of espionage' and on 2 September 1942 the Special Board of NKVD sentenced him to a further eight years in a corrective labour camp. He died of unknown causes while serving this sentence. Ivan Sukhanov was rehabilitated on both counts in 1957 and 1958.

Mikhail (Misha) Sukhanov graduated from the Moscow Architectural Institute in 1942 and went to fight at the front. After the war he, like his father, became an artist and architect. He lived his life in keeping with his father's parting words of written advice:

> You will, I assure you, come to see the sense in working hard and conscientiously. The most important thing in life is to have a calling and to love your work. You must move resolutely towards your intended goal. Only he who works and strives diligently at something he loves can become a true master . . . you must take action, you must work, and you must never give up. Misfortune may come knocking once, twice, even three times, but this does not mean that you need lose heart and stop working.

Mikhail Sukhanov died in Malakhovka in March 2018 at

the age of a hundred. The same address is still written on the gate: Shkolnaya Street, 2. There is a cheery cockerel-shaped weathervane on the roof, and beside the house, birches and pine trees that he planted with his father in 1931 grow proudly up towards the sky.

Boris Shustov

*'My first thought when I wake, and last when I fall asleep,
is of you, my darling daughter.'*

This chapter is taken from the memoirs of Boris Shustov's daughter, Inna Shustova. She writes:

My memoirs are based upon a folder containing a collection of letters that were carefully collected and filed away some years ago. My father, Boris Shustov (1902–68), gave the folder to me in the mid 1960s, shortly before his death. He had been arrested in 1938 in accordance with Article 58-10 and sentenced to five

Boris Shustov, Moscow, 1930

years' imprisonment and a three-year deprivation of civil rights.

I was born on 14 December 1932. By the time my father was arrested in 1938, my parents had divorced and formed new families. In 1940 my mother died, leaving me in the care of my stepfather. Unbeknown to me, my father had begun to look for me while in prison and each stage of his tireless search is reflected in the letters that he later gave me. I consider it my duty to preserve the memory of this remarkable man.

My father was born into a circle of people that had been decimated by the Revolution, having been labelled 'counter-revolutionaries', 'whites' and 'enemies of the people'. He was just fifteen when revolution gripped Russia and did not consider himself a member of any one of these 'subversive' groups. Nevertheless, had it not been for the ill health of his elder sister, which shattered their plans to emigrate, he and his family would certainly have left Russia during the Civil War.

Before the Revolution, the Shustov family had lived in a private house in St Petersburg. A German nursery governess was hired to take care of the four-year-old Boris and his two sisters: Zhenya, six, and two-year-old Nina. The governess did not speak a word of Russian and for a long time the children shied away from any form of communication with her. Nevertheless, like it or not, they were under her constant supervision and after two months all were babbling away happily in German.

At the end of his life my father mentioned that he was as comfortable thinking in German as he was in Russian; both came easily to him. Before the First World War he had managed to spend some time in Germany, where the architecture, in particular the Gothic style, had made a deep impression upon him. He carried this interest and love of traditional German culture with him throughout his life and read the works of Kant, Nietzsche, Schopenhauer and Hegel in their originals. My father loved Goethe and Heine's poetry, as well as music by Bach, Beethoven and Wagner. He was deeply troubled by fascism and was quick to recognise the common features it shared with Stalinism. Indeed, he once remarked with bitter irony that there had been one positive outcome of his arrest: he had been spared the torture of having to kill any Germans. It must also be said that his incarceration had another positive outcome – as strange as it may seem, my father became a better and kinder person. He saw the suffering of innocent people and in helping them, he experienced first-hand the intrinsic power of mutual assistance.

My father told us that our grandmother, Ekaterina

Vasiliyevna, had been born into an established noble family, but oddly he never mentioned her maiden name. It later transpired that after the Revolution, both she and her sister had made a vow never to reveal their ancestral family name to their children. However, one fact is known for certain: my father's father, Sergei Shustov, was a high-level official involved in the management of Russian Railways. My sister, Ksana, once asked my father who we might have been had the Revolution not occurred. Laughing playfully, he replied part in jest and part seriously, 'Well, at the very least you would have been the daughters of a Governor.'

Having been unable to emigrate, the Shustov family found themselves stranded in Sochi. It was decided that Boris should be sent away on an accountancy course; a practical choice based on the fact that no matter what the regime, accountants are always in demand. This notion proved correct, as evidenced by the fact that my father always managed to find reliable, albeit modest, work. Accountancy soothed him. Indeed, he often said that when he balanced an account, he also achieved mental equilibrium, which brought him peace. Moreover, specialising as an accountant meant that his thoughts were not occupied with matters of work outside of office hours, and therefore he was able to read in peace, compose poems, and study when at home. As a result, my father successfully taught himself history, philosophy and history of art.

He was travelling through Saratov in 1925 when he met the woman who was later to become my mother. She was the daughter of a city gardener and her name was Galina Zimina. They married three years later, and I was born in 1932.

My parents' married life did not prove to be straightforward and in 1935 my mother left my father for another man, Alexei Smakovsky. She took me with her and I grew up firm in the belief that Smakovsky was my biological father. I remembered 'Papa Borya' though. Before his arrest he would often come and visit me. He built houses out of blocks and filled them with wild animals made from paper, which he glued into animal shapes right there on the spot. A full performance would then play out before my very eyes. Above all, I loved it when he brought a plain exercise book of squared paper with him. Together we would trace pictures into it and for each picture he would think up a funny little rhyme and write it down next to our drawing in large capital letters. The result was a book that not a single other person possessed; it was mine and mine alone.

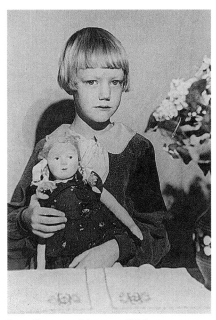

I loved reading, and began to learn before I had even turned five. It was Papa Borya who got me hooked on reading too. He would eagerly read aloud to me and loved listening, or at least gave the impression that he loved to listen, when I read!

Inna Shustova, Moscow, 1936.

Nevertheless, I must stress that I considered Smakovsky to be my biological father, and when my mother died in 1940 I continued to live with him, completely unaware that my real father had been arrested and imprisoned in a labour camp.

My father later told me about the circumstances of his arrest. He explained that by day he worked as an account inspector at the People's Commissariat of the Coal Industry, but in the evenings he wrote poems and attended a literary circle that met at people's homes. There, amateur poets read their poems to each other and shared their thoughts and impressions. Poetry was the only thing of importance in this circle; no other subject was ever touched upon. My father also read his poems aloud at these meetings, and was considered to be an Acmeist.* One day, a member of the circle whose name my father never mentioned, read out a poem that voiced, to put it mildly, dissatisfaction with his current existence and expressed a nostalgia for the past. The leader of the poetry circle suggested that they refrain from discussing the content of the poem, so the members limited their discourse to an analysis of its form, of which they were complimentary for the most part. The leader of the circle and the amateur poet in question were arrested the following day. Their phone books were seized and found to contain the names of each member of the poetry circle; my father's included.

Later, my father would respond to the interrogator's question of, 'Do you know why you have been arrested?' with a few lines of Gumilev's poetry:

> Because, these hands, these fingers,
> are frail, have never known a plough –
> Because songs, those everlasting gypsies,
> have come to me only in pain, ringing, dark[†]

In answer he received a kick to the right side of his jaw, which knocked out almost half of his teeth. When my father got to

---

* Translator's Note: Acmeism was an anti-Symbolist poetry movement that emerged in Russia in the early 1900s. Clarity, formal technique and a strong emphasis on the realistic and everyday characterise this school of poetry. Notable Acmeist poets include Anna Akhmatova, Osip Mandelstam and Nikolai Gumilev. In her book *Nietzsche and Soviet Culture: Ally and Adversary*, Glatzer Rosenthal explains that, 'because their emphasis on aesthetics, individualism and the primacy of the word conflicted with the tendencies of Soviet politics and culture, the movement was proscribed under Stalin. Gumilev was executed by the Bolsheviks in 1921 [and] Mandelstam died in a Stalinist camp.' (Cambridge University Press, Cambridge, 1994).

† From Gumilev's poem 'My Thoughts', 1908: *Selected Works of Nikolai S. Gumilev*, Burton Raffel and Alla Burago (State University of New York Press, Albany, 1972).

his feet, spitting out clots of blood, the interrogator calmly and dispassionately repeated his question. My father's sense of irony remained sufficient for him to quote Gumilev once again:

> Most likely, in a former life,
> I cut the throats of Mum and Dad.*

These lines cost him the teeth on the other side of his mouth. He lost consciousness. When they brought him round, the interrogator, who my father believed was now looking at him with a degree of sympathy, said something like, 'Do you really think we have time to work out whether or not you are guilty? Nobody is going to fiddle about with your case. We have hundreds just like you. Sign the confession or we will bring in your wife and mother.'

My father could not bear the thought of his loved ones suffering because of him. Mustering his strength, he walked over to the table and, without pausing to read it, signed his name on the piece of paper that the interrogator was pushing towards him with a look of relief. He was led away.

My father was sentenced to two years in prison and three years in a corrective labour camp. There were, however, more interrogations to come – the authorities hoped to make him betray his fellow members of the poetry circle. He was not allowed to sleep; they forced him to stay standing for several days and nights in a row. He later said that this was the hardest torture of all. The entire lower half of his body swelled enormously and caused him such pain that he regularly lost consciousness. But still he did not denounce anybody and it appears that he became so weak that they stopped interrogating him. He never knew what he had been charged with and, for the most part, it was of little interest to him even during the rehabilitation years. As

---

* Translation from Gumilev's poem 'Shame', 1917.

far as I know, my father died before receiving his rehabilitation certificates, but he considered himself to be innocent and his conscience was always clear. Following Stalin's death in 1953, he moved to Riga where nobody showed the slightest interest in this former chapter of his life.

My father always had his own views on history. He had a profound understanding of philosophy and read not only Marxist works, but also those of Marxism's critics. He believed that Stalin's regime of terror was a natural continuation of the Revolution and explained to me that it was this realistic understanding of all that had occurred that ultimately saved his sanity. In prison he met diehard revolutionaries and staunch Party supporters who simply could not acknowledge what had happened and believed that the authorities had been infiltrated by fascists who were deceiving Stalin. The minds of these physically strong and healthy people could not withstand their circumstances, and they invariably went mad.

My father could talk endlessly about the years he had spent in prison and in the camps. However, when I was a child he spared my innocent mind, keeping silent about many aspects of prison life. Later he told me that when he arrived in the camp after his years in prison, it was the women who made the most striking impression upon him: he had not heard a woman's voice for two whole years. The camp 'beauties' swore obscenely but he heard only the 'heavenly music' of their voices and intonation.

At the camp, my father was saved from the grind of hard labour by the urki.* He was an excellent storyteller and always respectful of anyone he talked to, regardless of his status. The criminals nicknamed him 'White Swan' and they made it his duty to be their Scheherazade, narrating part of a continuing story every evening. He weaved together a fantastical web of Bret Harte, James Fenimore Cooper, Walter Scott, Jack London,

---

* Common criminals (see footnote on page 69).

Anatole France, Graham Greene and even Laclos; entertaining the urki with extraordinary tales of adventure. In return, the criminals would give him demos of their professional craft, inconspicuously pilfering whatever they liked from the pockets of their neighbours. My father marvelled unreservedly at their tricks, which they found rather flattering. But most importantly, as a result of his wonderful storytelling, the criminals helped him to fulfil his work quota, both building railways and felling trees in his name. Being physically weak, my father would not have withstood this work without their assistance.

The camp was hit by harsh frosts, with temperatures plummeting to minus thirty degrees Celsius, and my father contracted pneumonia. He was taken to the camp infirmary, where a free woman [non-prisoner], who I believe worked in the canteen, saved him from certain death. My father was forever grateful to her and affectionately called her 'Shurochka'. She fed and nursed him back to health, and it appears that she developed a genuine affection for him, to the extent that when my father turned a corner and his health improved, Shurochka fought to secure him a job in the hospital, as an account-keeper, if I'm not mistaken.

I was about fourteen years old when my father first told me that, 'there will come a time when it will no longer be those in prison or in exile who are shamed, but those who allowed this to happen. We will be considered heroes . . . This will happen in your lifetime.'

However, the bright spark of Khrushchev's 'thaw'* arrived in time for my father to witness it too. He rejoiced in the fact that the truth had surfaced, but said that the past had been pierced by a needle so tiny that only the smallest trickle of truth could possibly seep out of the opening. He wholeheartedly welcomed Solzhenitsyn's *One Day in the Life of Ivan Denisovich* but considered it to be first and foremost a literary work,

---

* After Stalin's death, there was a softening in the Soviet regime and criticism of Stalin's personality cult.

albeit a factual one. 'Camp life was a hundred times worse,' he said. My father did not manage to read Solzhenitsyn's other titles. He had hinted that he had a finished book charting his own life mapped out in his head, but he decided not to write it. He feared that the past could repeat itself and was cautious about his actions. His personal files contain only fragments, hints and isolated chapters broken off at the most interesting parts.

So let us return to the letters enclosed in the file that my father gave me before he died. Having found out while in the camp that Alexei Smakovsky had decided to officially adopt me, he wrote the following letter to the Custodial Council in the Frunzenskaya region of Moscow:

From Boris Sergeyevich Shustov
Koryazhma. Arkhangelsk Region
P.O. Box 219/3

My former wife, Galina Nikolayevna Shustova-
Smakovskaya (née Zimina), died on 25 February 1940.
She is survived by a seven-year-old daughter named Inna,
who is currently living with her stepfather, the deceased's
second husband, Alexei Konstantinovich Smakovsky.
[. . .] It has come to my knowledge that Smakovsky
intends to use my enforced absence (I am a prisoner in a
corrective labour camp) to adopt my daughter against my
will. As the child's father, I not only have not and will
not give my consent to this adoption, but I emphatically
protest against it [. . .]. I am currently residing at the
Sevzheldorlag, in the 7th work battalion of the 3rd
division, and as a prisoner I have been deprived of the
ability to retrieve my daughter and provide her with a
home. Under no circumstances, however, will I surrender
my parental rights and at the very first opportunity I will

address the burning matter of returning my daughter to my care, in accordance with current legislation.

Shustov
1 September 1940

On the very same day that my father wrote this letter I was attending my first day at school, completely unaware of his fate. His camp prison sentence would end in 1943 but as a consequence of his having been deprived of his civil rights he was banned from returning to Moscow. Nevertheless, as soon as he was released from prison, he began to search for me.

An extract from a letter to A. Smakovsky from Boris Shustov:

Alexei Konstantinovich! [. . .] It has come to my attention that you have recently remarried. My spell of ordeals is now over and I am currently working as head accountant on one of the main NKVD building projects. I am wholly financially secure and would like to bring my daughter Innochka to live with me. [. . .] I am once again in a position to support, raise and surround my daughter with love.

You, Alexei Konstantinovich, have found family happiness for the second time. After many calamitous years, including the death of my mother and other family members, the opportunity to take back my daughter would bring me great solace. For this reason, I hope that you will not refuse to share your thoughts with me on this sensitive matter. I eagerly await your response.

Shustov
25 January 1944

Events then unfurled in a way that nobody could possibly

have predicted. My father unexpectedly received a response to his letter, not from Smakovsky, but from our neighbour, affectionately known as Auntie Valya. In it she wrote that my stepfather beat me (this was true), that I was 'very unhappy' (I didn't feel particularly unhappy), that I remembered 'Papa Borya' and that he needed to rescue me and so on . . .

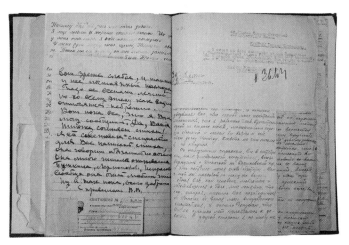

The folder of letters belonging to Boris Shustov, which he gave to his daughter Irina shortly before his death.

My father replied at once – he was interested in any string that he could grasp and use to track me down. An exchange of letters ensued. Smakovsky and I had moved into a different apartment with his new wife, but Auntie Valya eventually found me and handed me a letter from my father. Unfortunately, he did not keep copies of all of his letters and the originals have not survived. But my father did file my response and a copy of his subsequent letter under 'affairs'.

> My dear Papa Borya!
> I received your letter. I am so happy that you have turned
> up! I think about you every day. You ask how my life is.
> When I was about eight years old Papa often hit me for
> very minor things (even our friends said so). For the past

year things have been better and we have been getting on well. Papa looks after me very well and really loves me. I would gladly come and live with you, but I would feel sorry for my Papa. I love him a lot too (though I love you more), and I would feel bad leaving him. I can't tell you how much I want to see you. From 1 October I will be back at school – I will be going into the afternoon session of Year 5. Come to Moscow if you can. At the moment Papa's duties mean that he always has to go away on business trips. He wants to hire somebody. So come and live with us for forever and ever. I think that Papa would agree to it. Write and tell me if Grandmother Katya is still alive and where you are living. If you are not too far away then maybe you could come and collect me during the holidays and I could spend them with you. Send me your photograph. I am sending you a big, big kiss.

Your Inna

My father replied quickly:

My darling Innochka!
Today is a happy day. I have found you, received a letter from you, and discovered that you are alive, healthy and living much better than I had feared was the case.

It has been a year since I wrote to Alexei Konstantin- ovich at Barykovsky Lane and told him that I was looking for you, but I never received an answer. I waited for month after month, utterly despondent. And then suddenly today I receive a letter from you! But today is not in fact the happiest day of my life – that day will come when I see you again, my dear daughter. I don't live so very far away – four days from Moscow by train. But now it is wartime and everyone must man his post,

so it will be very difficult for me to obtain permission
to come and visit you. Nevertheless, I am already busy
trying to arrange a visit and perhaps I will manage to
come and see you during the holidays. In the meantime,
we will write to each other. Write to me often, little one.
Let me know whether you are eating well and who is
cooking for you at the moment. Tell me what school you
are attending. You write so well and so coherently that I
have decided to write you a letter in my normal cursive
handwriting, rather than using printed letters.

Granny Katya has not forgotten you, but she passed
away, which is why she has not come to visit. But don't
be sad, Innochka. Remember that I love you more than
anyone on this earth. You are always in my thoughts. My
first thought when I wake, and last when I fall asleep, is of
you, my darling daughter.

Your Papa Borya

Convinced that I remembered, loved and would like to live
with him, my father sought to obtain leave from work in order
to come and visit me. Instead of a leave of absence, he received
the following response:

Urdoma Station
Northern–Pechorsky Railway
Post Office: Nyanda
To: Shustov

In response to your application for leave addressed to
Deputy People's Commissar, Comrade Safrazyan, the
personnel department of the GULZHDS* NKVD USSR

* Main Camp Directorate for Railway Construction of the NKVD (MVD).

informs you that at the current time it is not possible to grant you leave to travel to Moscow.

Head of GULZHDS NKVD USSR, Zamotaev.

30 September 1944

My father put his zealous and analytical mind to work and came up with a plan, the essence of which he outlined in a letter to Smakovsky:

Alexei Konstantinovich!

On 25 January 1944 I sent a letter to your Barikovsky address in which I informed you that the challenging spell in my life has come to an end and that I am now employed in the position of head accountant on one of the NKVD's building projects. I am financially secure and would like to take back my daughter Innochka. I did not receive an answer to this letter. [. . .] Not only is looking after Innochka my primary duty as her biological and legal father, but it is also my ardent desire. [. . .]

The bearer of this letter, a worker from our company by the name of Ivan Mikhailovich Nikitin, is carrying with him all the necessary travel documents and will bring my daughter to me. Innochka loves and remembers me and I think that she will come willingly. There is a secondary school here where she can continue her studies.

Regards,
Shustov
22 October 1944

At the same time my father began to prepare a letter to me:

My darling Innochka!

The chap who brought you this letter will be leaving in ten days' time. He can take you back with him, my dear, and bring you to me. He will come to you in ten days' time and you can tell him whether or not you would like to go with him. If you would like to come then you will need to speak to Alexei Konstantinovich – I have written to him as well. I will meet you here and we will live together. There is a school here where you can continue your studies. I am sending you a big, big kiss, my beloved daughter, and hope to see you here very, very soon.

Your Papa Borya

From this point on, events played out much like a tragicomedy, causing a huge amount of worry and stress to everyone involved. Fearing that Smakovsky would not let me go to Papa Borya, and that he would punish me severely for asking, I ran away. I took with me my favourite doll, a small pack of semolina porridge and some bread ration cards. I left Smakovsky a note that I had written myself, entirely of my own accord: 'I have gone to live with my father and will not be coming back to see you ever again.' Naturally, I was found and brought back to Moscow. Smakovsky and my father began to exchange letters.

In a letter to my father dated 4 December 1944 Smakovsky said:

If you recall, the question of paternity was always ambiguous. You will also remember that on one occasion when we met it was agreed that we would look into this issue a little later, when Inna was older. If you insist that we have now reached this point, then first and foremost I would like to see you. I would have thought that we might together be able to ascertain her paternity somehow, whether by establishing blood types or by using some other method. But I repeat that I do not wish to worry the child with this matter until this question has been settled definitively. For this reason I ask that you desist from communicating with her further and from sending anyone else to act on your behalf . . .

In a letter to Smakovsky dated 30 December 1944 my father said:

. . . I have never been in any doubt as to Inna's paternity. I have always considered (and still consider) her to be my daughter beyond all shadow of a doubt. [. . .] I am ready to discuss any reservations that you might have and to perform blood tests of any sort. That said, the matter of my visiting Moscow has become more problematic on two counts: firstly in view of the fact that it has become extremely difficult to obtain permission to travel to the capital and secondly due to the no lesser challenge of being granted leave from work. In any case, I will do all that I can to surmount these obstacles . . .

My father was nervous. The plan to visit Moscow did not come to fruition and my stepfather threatened to take the case to court. In the end, my father had no choice but to ask his second wife, Victoria, to take me in until he could get to Moscow. She demurred, not relishing the prospect of looking after a stepdaughter alongside a daughter of her own. In despair, and after much contemplation, my father decided to write to the director of the school I attended:

Comrade School Director,
Following a great deal of thought about who might

be able to help me, I have decided to turn to you. As
the director of a Soviet school, and perhaps as a parent
yourself, you will understand my situation.

In Class 5B at your school there is a child called
Innochka Shustova (Smakovsky). I am her biological
father, both legally and by birth.

. . . If you were able to send Innochka to me at once, I
would pay all of the costs for a teacher to accompany her
(it is a 3.5 day journey on a direct train from Kurskaya
Station). If this matter goes to court, I will send a letter
of attorney either to you, to a lawyer or to another
individual whom you may recommend.

I enclose 300 roubles with this letter. Please spend it as
you see fit on textbooks for Innochka, extra school food;
in short, on anything that you consider she needs.

I hope that I can rely on your help.

Shustov

In the spring of 1944 I was confidently awaiting a change in
my fate.

A child welfare inspector arrived to check that the conditions
in which I was living corresponded to those described in a letter
from my father. He asked me, 'Inna, would you like to go and
live with Shustov or stay with Smakovsky?'

Scared silly by both his arrival and the question, I got cold
feet. Glancing over at my stepfather who was leafing idly
through some book, affecting not to be paying the slightest bit
of attention to me, I mumbled, 'Stay.'

Tension hovered in the air, but it seemed that the inspector
had picked up on my fear.

'And what if you have a little think about it?' he asked gently.

'Leave,' I muttered in a voice that was barely audible.

My fate was decided. From that moment on, every day as I
walked home from school I would look into the faces of the

men walking past and try to guess whether one of them was my father, arriving to take me home with him.

Inna Shustova with her father, Boris Shustov, 1946.

We were reunited on the 21 May 1945, when my father came to Moscow. Ten days later he took me to the small village of Urdoma in the Arkhangelsk region, where he was working as chief supervisor in the administrative department for the Northern Railway Corrective Labour Camp (Sevzheldorlag).

On the 24 November 1991 I wrote to the Military Procurator of the Supreme Court of the Soviet Union seeking restorative justice and requesting that they re-examine my father's case. I received a response from the Procurator General of the Russian Federation stating that my father would be rehabilitated fully on 30 September 1994.

Inna Borisovna Shustova graduated from the Philology Faculty of the Krupskaya Moscow Regional Pedagogical Institute. She worked for several publishing houses including Gizlegprom (State Publishing House for Light Industry), Pedagogia and Znaniye, where she ran the scientific department. Inna also wrote several books herself, including a memoir, *Smoke Shadows*, and a number of books for children.

Gavriil Gordon

'If these few pages can help you to find your way in life,
I will be very happy indeed.'

Gavriil Gordon died from star-vation in the Volga Corrective Labour Camp (Volgolag) in 1942. He left behind two exercise books for his daughters, Elizaveta and Irina, each filled from cover to cover with tiny handwriting. On the cover of the first book was written, 'A little introduction to big philosophy for my sweet Likunechka.' This exercise book was intended for his elder daughter, Elizaveta. The second was entitled, 'A Short

Gavriil Gordon, Morshansk, 1910.

Introduction to the Study of History for my sweet daughter Irina.' At the time Gordon wrote these in 1937 Elizaveta (affectionately known as Likunechka) was seventeen and Irina thirteen years old.

While serving time in a labour camp in 1937 Gordon penned 'A Short Story about My Life', an unfinished autobiographical narrative, the manuscript of which is currently on display in the Pushkin State Museum of Fine Arts. Further information on Gordon's life can also be found in the memoirs of the prominent

Gavriil Gordon with his wife, Elizaveta, and daughters Elizaveta and Irina. This photograph was taken during a visit they made to the Solovki labour camp, 1931.

intellectual Dmitry Likhachov*, who served a sentence in the Solovki camp alongside Gordon in the early 1930s, and in those of Gordon's son Georgiy (Yuri) who writes about a visit to his father at the camp on the Solovetsky Islands in 1931.[†] Kristina Mironova's 2012 PhD thesis 'Gavriil Osipovich Gordon in the History of Russian Neo-Kantianism'[‡] was also dedicated to its eponymous character.

Gavriil Gordon was born on 8 May 1885 in the city of Spassk in the Tambov Governorate. His parents were district council pharmacists[§] and in 1890 the family moved to Moscow,

---

* Dmitry S. Likhachov, *Reflections on the Russian Soul: A Memoir* (St Petersburg: Logos), 1995.

† G. Gordon. 'Journey to Solovki' in the *Solovetsky Vestnik*, January–February 1995, No. 90–5.

‡ Mironova, K., *Gavriil Osipovich Gordon in the History of Russian Neo-Kantianism* (Saratov State University, 2012).

§ Translator's note: Also called 'zemsky pharmacists'. The name is derived from the word 'Zemstvo' which was given to the local district councils that appeared in rural Russia between 1864 and 1918. The doctors and pharmacists affiliated to these councils provided a medical service for Russia's rural population and sought to educate and improve public health standards in their districts.

where the young Gavriil finished his studies at the gymnasium with a silver medal.* In 1909, he graduated from Moscow University's History and Philology Department, succeeding in adding another silver medal to his name. Between 1906 and 1907 he took a course in Germany called 'Summer Sessions on Philosophy' at Marburg University, which was led by the founders of the Marburg school of Neo-Kantianism: Hermann Cohen and Paul Natorp.

While completing his teacher-training course in Moscow, Gordon paid his way by teaching ancient history and tutoring the family of the famous art collector and merchant Sergei Shchukin. In 1911, he married Elizaveta Voskresenskaya, the granddaughter of the Archpriest of Morshansk Cathedral. At the time, Elizaveta was studying at the then recently established Moscow Courses of Higher Education for Women.

In 1914, just before the outbreak of the war, Gordon embarked on a tour of the historical sites of Greece and Turkey. When the First World War struck, Gordon enlisted, and between 1914 and 1916 he served as commander of the 55th Reserve Regiment. In 1917 he was stationed on the front line just outside the city of Baranavichy,† where he served as squadron commander before being transferred in August to the intelligence section at the headquarters of the Grenadier Corps. In 1918, Gordon was chosen by his fellow soldiers to be a member of the delegation sent to negotiate a ceasefire with the Germans at a section of the front line near Baranavichy. Once the peace treaty had been finalised, he returned to his family in Morshansk, where he was appointed head of the town's Department of Public Education. He became a member of the Communist Party of the Soviet Union in 1919,

---

* Translator's note: Silver and gold medals were awarded to the students who obtained the highest marks across all of their subjects. Achieving a medal significantly improved a child's chances of being admitted into a competitive institute of higher education.
† Today this city is in Belarus.

was mobilised into the Red Army, and joined the Morshansk Revolutionary Committee. A little later, he was redeployed to the military headquarters at Tambov. When the Civil War ended, Gordon became a professor at Tambov University, where he founded the Science and Philosophy Society.

A dazzling career in Moscow followed his military and academic success. Gordon became a board member of the People's Commissariat for Education of the Russian Soviet Federative Socialist Republic, and a close ally of Nadezhda Krupskaya (Lenin's wife). In addition to this, he became deputy chairman of the Council of Higher Education and joined the teaching department at the State Science Council. He taught at Moscow State University (I and II), giving lectures on logic in the Social Science Faculty and teaching courses on education at the Pedagogical Faculty. He also taught a course on the history of revolutionary movements in Europe at Sverdlov Communist University and wrote several history textbooks including *The Chartist Movement*, *The Revolution of 1848* and *The History of Class War in the West*. Besides all this, he also engaged in some publishing work.

Gavriil Gordon was one of those people whose talents were plain for all to see. The sheer depth and scope of his knowledge was astounding. He was a philosopher, philologist, historian, musical expert and teacher. Dmitry Likhachov described him as 'astonishingly well-educated'. In his biography, Gavriil's son writes that by the age of fifteen, Gordon had read all of the historical annals published at that time and housed in the State Historical Museum library. As a student, he read all the works of the Ancient Greek playwrights and prose writers in their originals, in addition to the French and German classics and the works of eighteenth- and nineteenth-century philosophers such as Spinoza, Kant, Hegel and Marx.

He was also a keen amateur pianist. He studied all of the founding literary material on music history in Russian, German and French and in 1924 he took up a two-year post teaching history of music at the Gnessin Musical College, known at that time as the Third Moscow Musical School.

Gordon had a profound impact upon the system of Soviet education, devising the methodological framework for the Polytechnic Workers School and advocating the importance of educating people about world cultures and giving theoretical training in such schools, rather than focusing purely on industrial matters. Contrary to the dominant view in the 1920s that only a general programme of social sciences ought to be taught in schools, Gordon insisted that it was imperative to adopt measures to enable the teaching of history as an independent subject. He co-founded a publishing house called The Worker's Enlightenment, where he oversaw the publication of the periodicals *Teaching Courses at Home* and *The Pedagogical University at Home*. These essentially became the first examples of remote educational materials for teacher training in the USSR.

As Likhachov later wrote:

> No amount of information, either in articles or textbooks, could equal the vast scope of his knowledge. He had mastered Ancient Greek and German perfectly, knew French and Latin well, spoke fluent Italian, and could read in English, Spanish, Swedish and all the Slavic languages. He strove constantly to learn something new and even while imprisoned in the Solovki camp, he seized the opportunity to learn Arabic from a fellow prisoner, a mufti from the Moscow Cathedral Mosque. In return, he gave the mufti lessons in Ancient Greek.

From his son's memoirs, we also learn that Gordon was

> a wonderful lecturer and expressive speaker, who delivered his talks without notes and spoke with great clarity,

cadence and imagination. He never complicated his science unnecessarily, and could connect with any audience at all. [. . .] He was a good horseman, a skilled shot and a talented chess player, and is said to have played the grand piano so well that famous pianists sat down to play duets with him. He was very demanding of those around him but exceptionally unselfish, decent, and honest to the point of naivety. [. . .] He was an amiable man and had many very close friends, but it proved even easier to make enemies, living as he was among people who envied his talents and decency.

What could this man have expected from Soviet Russia? Sergei Larkov, a modern historian and author of a biographical article on Gordon, astutely observed that 'Such people did not fit in with the new Soviet community. They were irredeemably individual, irritatingly bright, and sickeningly talented. Their fates had been decided long ago and they were walking the road to Calvary.'*

Gordon was arrested for the first time in the autumn of 1929. An OGPU panel charged him with espionage and sentenced him to ten years in a corrective labour camp in accordance with Article 58-6. He served his sentence at a camp on the Solovetsky Islands in the White Sea.

Dimitry Likhachov writes in his memoirs:

> Despite the fact that Gordon never truly found his place in life, no matter where he turned up, his presence was always hugely valued. As soon as he arrived at the camp, my young circle of friends offered to help him. Before long, he was welcomed into the fold of the 'artistic set' and earned a place in the camp Criminology Cabinet.† We later took measures

---

* Sergei Larkov, *Introduction to Life and Extermination from Life*, 30 October 2002, No. 23.

† A scientific institution founded by the criminologist A. Kolosov. The KrimKab, as it was known, was tasked with investigating crimes within the camp.

to ensure that he didn't stand out too much: he didn't line up in the first row during roll call, and in the corridors of the camp administration he spoke very quietly. But even from the back row he managed to come out with two or three sharp ripostes in response to the tedious admonitory lectures given by Commander A. Kunst during roll call. These remarks (he would often ask pertinent questions or play along with the lecture just to highlight the stupidity of what Kunst was saying) had a tendency to enrage the idiot-commanders, and Kunst, although cunning and sly, wasn't renowned for his intelligence.

For the youngsters at Solovki, Gordon became a university of sorts. Not only did he give them coaching on any topic of their choosing, but remarkably, he was also able to improvise lectures for a couple of them, even citing precise quotes or bibliographical references and reciting poems. Perhaps most importantly, he could cite crucial sections from Goethe's 'Faust' in German. This was a play in which we were all very interested at the time . . . The young people at Solovki were drawn to the spontaneous and jovial Gavriil, and though he was open and uninhibited, he would never show off (as is always tempting for a teacher to do). He was forever getting mixed up in some trouble or other, and this attracted enemies, which carried with it enormous risk at that time . . .

In 1931, Gordon's sentence was commuted to five years in exile in Sverdlovsk.* There he worked as a consultant methodologist in the Regional Department for Public Education and wrote a geography textbook for secondary school children.

Below are a few extracts from letters that he sent home to his daughters from Sverdlovsk:

---

* Today Yekaterinburg.

Sweet Likunechka,

I received your postcard yesterday. You ask whether I received the package of books. Everything arrived and I wrote to tell you so, but it appears that you did not receive my letter. If the textbook is printed, I will send it to both you and Irina – it might prove useful. You are now old enough to read 'War and Peace'. Why is it that you are hoping to see me in a month, or even two weeks' time?

I would never have guessed the homonym (not *ha monym* as you wrote) without your clue: I have grown stupid. I am very bored without you, and without Irochka, your mama, Yuri and Auntie Alya.

Write to me often – I really love to read your notes. I am sending you a big kiss on your ears and snout. Papa.

Sweet Irochka,

Thank you for the letter that you dictated to Auntie Alya for me. I had some visitors a few days ago – Murzilka, Doctor Maz-Peremaz, Tom Thumb, Little Kroshechka and The Tailor and The Merchant.* I fed them a drop of honey and some breadcrumbs. We talked about you and they promised to visit you too. They are only able to visit at night though, so make sure you don't miss them! Write and tell me how you are doing at school. I am sending you a big kiss. Give Mama and Auntie Alya a kiss from me. Papa. (22.09.1932)

Sweet Likunya,

Yesterday I received your postcard dated 26 December and I am overjoyed to hear that you passed your music exam so well. I am also very pleased that you have been

---

* These names refer to a selection of characters from Russian children's books and fairy tales.

given good pieces to play. There is so much wonderful music on this earth; compositions by Bach, Mozart, Handel, Beethoven and other great composers, so there is no need for you to play anything second-rate. Schumann wrote down some guidelines for young musicians to follow. He advised them to play proper, quality music and not to spoil their taste with various lousy waltzes, polkas, gallops and other such rubbish. So I too am happy to hear that you are studying Bach, Handel and Mozart rather than 'A Maiden's Prayer' (ask your mother about this one – she knows this third-rate piece by Madame Bondazhevskaya* well). I have one small comment to make: you think that the cat is a 'relashion'† of the lynx, but it is in fact a 'relation'. But I am sending you a big, big kiss on your little nose and ears. Give Irochka a kiss from me, and Mummy, Yuri and Auntie Alya too. I love you very much. Papa. (03.01.1933)

The 29th day of the month of April, 1933.
In the city of Yekaterinburg, now Sverdlovsk.

My Gracious Lady and Benefactress, Elizaveta Gavriilovna!
If I may be so bold, I would like to bring to your kind attention an excellent little book about a certain French musician: a gentleman by the name of François Gossec, who toiled tirelessly for the duration of his long life. I entreat you not to take offence, but if I may be so bold, I shall hasten to send you a small dictionary to assist in the understanding of the book. I hereby wish to draw your gracious attention to the fact that the gentleman

---

* Polish composer Tekla Badarzewska.
† Little Elizaveta had emitted the letter 't' from the Russian work 'rodstvennik' meaning 'relation'.

who penned the book in question filled it with a great
many expressions that are not always easy to understand.
I await with great anticipation your esteemed opinion on
the book. I miss you and your mother a great deal, not to
mention that dear brother and sister of yours, from whom
I have not received any letters in some considerable time.
Oh, how miserable my life is, so far from those sweetest
and dearest to my heart. That said, My Gracious Lady
and Benefactress, I am honoured to remain forever more
your humble servant and parent and hope very much that
Fortune, that most kind Roman goddess, will bestow her
blessing upon us.

Would you be so kind as to kiss your Mama, brother,
sister and esteemed Auntie Olga Alexandrovna a hundred
times for me.

PS. Send my deepest regards to your chicken – I wish her
the very best of health.

Having been freed from exile ahead of schedule in 1933,
Gavriil Gordon returned to Moscow, where he took up a post
teaching history in a school and translating literature for the
publishing house Academia.

His freedom was short-lived. He was arrested again on 31 July
1936 – it transpired that one of his colleagues at Academia had
informed against him. The NKVD were handed a statement
by Gordon in reference to the Stalin constitution,* which was
a topic of much speculation at that time. Gordon was alleged
to have said, 'The Constitution will be a document of great
significance in the history of mankind providing it does not
prove to be a bluff.' He was sentenced by the Special Board of

---

* A new constitution was adopted in 1936, cementing Socialist-Realism as the
reigning ideology in the USSR. It became known, unofficially, as the Stalin
Constitution.

NKVD to five years in a corrective labour camp on the charge of 'anti-Soviet agitation and propaganda' in accordance with Article 58-10. He served his sentence at the Volgolag, where he worked as a guard on the Uglich Hydroelectric Station during its construction. It was thanks to the considerable efforts of Nadezhda Krupskaya that he ended up in this particular camp, not far from Moscow.

> My sweet Likunechka,
>
> I haven't written to you for a long time: it has been difficult. I have been very anxious to hear about your exams at the Music Academy though. How did you sing? I cannot wait to hear from you. I wanted to tell you something: when you have time, take my little book (on the shelf in the kitchen) by Anton Rubinstein* called 'Musik und Meister' (I think that's the title) and try to read it. It will be good practice for your German and above all, it is very well written despite being a little conservative in regard to music. It is a good type of conservatism though – refined in taste and with a deep understanding of music. Rubinstein (at this very moment – es nehme es der Teufel! – some bars from 'The Demon' played on the domra† and balalaika are crackling through the radio) was a great musician. Afterwards, if you can face it, have a look at 'Musikgeschichte Naumann'a', which you will also find in the kitchen, and pick out the most noteworthy chapters. It contains a lot of interesting drawings and was given to me by I. Shukin 28 years ago. Stay healthy, Sweetheart. Give your Mama, Irochka and Yuri a kiss from me. Things are all right with me for the

---

* Nineteenth-century Russian composer and founder of the St Petersburg Conservatory.

† A Russian (folk) musical instrument with a round body and three or four strings.

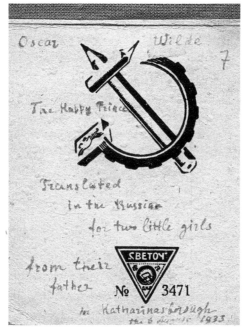

A translation of Oscar Wilde's 'The Happy Prince' by
Gavriil Gordon. On the cover is written in English:

Oscar Wilde
The Happy Prince
Translated in the Russian for two little girls.
From their father in Katharinas-borough.
1933

time being. I am sending you a big kiss and a hug. Papa
(21.08.1937)

While working on the construction of the Uglich
Hydroelectric Station, Gordon also wrote a memoir entitled *A
Short Novel on my Life* as well as two books for his daughters:
An Introduction to Philosophy and *An Introduction to History*. The
latter two notebooks were addressed to his daughters, and the
knowledge and memory displayed by their author is astounding.
Despite not having a single book to hand, he quotes texts by
both foreign and pre-revolutionary Russian intellectuals almost
word for word, sometimes even in their original languages.

Addressing his daughter Elizaveta, Gordon writes:

Notebooks written for Elizaveta and Irina, 1937.

This exercise book was written in many different places: I either wrote it among the hubbub and swearing of the crowded office headquarters, or in the barracks at night, listening to the interchangeable snores of unfamiliar sleeping men. It was written during days of uncertainty and agonising suspense as I awaited new trials. But when I wrote it, my pen was moved by my great love for you, my sweet daughter. And in remembering my past philosophy lessons I was transported away from the crushing reality of my surroundings and into a world where I could enjoy the pure thoughts and reflections of wonderful bygone times which, along with music, always formed the true substance and sustenance of my 'self'. It is a small 'introduction' and by no means perfect. I wrote it without access to a single scientific essay (I don't have any here) and without doing a draft, but I hope that it gives you a few pointers as to what aspects of Philosophy should be of interest to you, if indeed it really does interest you. Of course, in the way that it is written and structured it must be said that it is a repository of my own, largely impressionistic way of thinking. I did, however, try to be objective and, in leaving everything unanswered, to give you an insight into the pluralism of Philosophy and the abundance of its problems . . .

. . . If these few pages can help you to find your way in life, I will be very happy indeed. (1937)

Unfortunately Elizaveta Gordon was not destined to continue finding her 'way'. She died suddenly in 1940, but her family did not have the heart to tell Gavriil the news.

In her memoirs Irina Gordon writes:

> Likunya, my elder sister, was my father's favourite. She died in 1940 aged nineteen, having just begun her second year at Moscow State University's Faculty of Mechanics and Mathematics. [. . .] My mother did not know how to break this news to my father and decided to conceal it from him until after his release. I wrote and told him that Lika had joined the Komsomol and had given her word that she would no longer maintain a relationship with her repressed father.[*]

Gavriil Gordon's sentence ended in August 1941, but as a consequence of the recent outbreak of war, he was not released on schedule. He died of starvation in the camp in January 1942.

In Georgiy Gordon's biography of his father, he makes a bitter calculation:

> Of the 32 years between his graduation from university and death in 1942, my father dedicated eight years to military service, spent eight years in labour camps, and two years in exile. As a consequence, he was able to fulfil only a tiny proportion of what a man with his abilities, education and love of science could have accomplished.

---

[*] The *Solovetsky Vestnik*, 1995, No. 1.

Gavriil Gordon was fully rehabilitated on 18 April 1957.

Georgiy Gordon (1911–87) graduated from the Moscow Institute of Geodetics and Cartography and became a design engineer. His younger daughter, Irina, graduated from the Philology Faculty of the Lomonosov Moscow State University and taught English in schools in Moscow for many years. In the late 1950s she became a professional English–Russian translator and went on to become a leading figure in the field of Russian literary translation. Her translated works comprise classic and modern oeuvres from across a wide range of genres. Irina died in Moscow in 2010 at the age of eighty-five.

Vladimir Levitsky

'I have only one wish — to see you again, and then die. I
need nothing more.'

Vladimir Levitsky (1873–1937) was arrested in Kursk in 1931 and sentenced to ten years in a corrective labour camp. He was sent to Siberia, from where he never returned; his sentence was modified and he was shot.

Vladimir Levitsky, Kiev, late 1890s.

During his time in Siberia, Levitsky sent more than two hundred letters home to Kursk, many of which were accompanied by his own drawings. The letters were addressed to his wife, Natalya (neé Levashkevich), and son, Oleg, or 'Olyusha', who was only fifteen years old at the time of his father's arrest. In 2009 Levitsky's granddaughter Natalya Petrovanova published the 149 letters that had been preserved in the family archives.[*]

Vladimir Levitsky was born into a family of village priests in

---

[*] The letters were published in *V. V. Levitsky: Letters from a Siberian Camp: A Documentary-Biographical Story*, compiled by N. O. Petrovanova (Oryol: Labour), 2009.

the small town of Russkaya Polyana in the Kiev Governorate.*
He attended the local gymnasium in Belaya Tserkov and went
on to study law at the Kiev University of Saint Vladimir† for
two years, before abandoning his studies in favour of a career in
the military. In 1895, Levitsky enrolled voluntarily as a private
in the 131st Tiraspol Infantry Regiment and before long he was
sent to the Kiev Junker Infantry Military Training College.‡

Within a year he had been promoted to the rank of Junker
officer, and after a further year he graduated with honours from
the military college. He was then promoted again, this time to the
rank of second lieutenant, and posted to the 129th Bessarabskiy
Infantry Regiment to continue his military service. By 1901,
Levitsky was a lieutenant serving as regimental aide-de-camp.

Later that year he was transferred to the 203rd Graivoronsky
Infantry Reserve Battalion, the headquarters of which were in
Kursk. It was there that the young lieutenant met his future
wife, Natalya, while visiting a tearoom owned by her father, a
merchant-trader called Levashkevich. They were married two
years later, in 1903.

The dependable and diligent Levitsky rose rapidly through the
ranks, from regimental adjutant, to staff captain and commandant
of the regimental training team, before finally becoming the
company commander. However, his military career took an
unexpected turn in 1905, when he was posted to the Orlov
Bakhtin Cadet Corps,§ which was in need of officer-teachers.

The years that Levitsky spent teaching at the Cadet Corps

---

* Today this is in Ukraine.

† Now the Taras Shevchenko National University of Kyiv.

‡ Junker schools in Russia prepared low-rank military personnel for the rank
of officer.

§ The Orlov Bakhtin Cadet Corps was a military training college for young
boys of noble descent. It was established in Oryol in 1843. It was named after
the former colonel and landowner in the Oryol and Kursk regions, Mikhail
Petrovich Bakhtin, who donated 1.5 million roubles and 2,700 of his peasants to
the building of the Cadet Corps.

Vladimir Levitsky with his young pupils at the Orlov Bakhtin Cadet Corps, 1910.

(1905–17) were to be the happiest of the young couple's lives. They had a lovely five-room apartment in the officers' quarters near the school's campus in Oryol, and the teaching work provided Levitsky with a good salary. Outside of work, he was able to find time to indulge in his favourite hobbies: painting, photography, and collecting coins and stamps. They enjoyed all the comforts of family life, even employing a maid. The year 1915 brought a long-awaited and joyful event: the birth of a son.

Vladimir Levitsky was a keen photographer, and in 1908 he became a member of the Oryol Photographic Society. More often that not, his photographic subjects were his cadet pupils. As an officer-teacher, he was delegated to accompany them on summer sightseeing excursions to various Russian cities, from the Crimea to the Caucasus, and with each one his family photo album expanded.

In 1912, Levitsky began a year-long course at the military training department headquarters in St Petersburg (he and his wife rented an apartment on Liteyny Avenue). The certificate that he received upon completing the course stated that he was permitted to teach penmanship, fencing and handicraft at Cadet Academies. In December 1913, he was promoted to lieutenant colonel and six months later was encouraged to travel to Italy as a member of a group of teachers on an academic (training exchange) assignment. He received a number of awards including the Order of St Stanislav (2nd and 3rd class), the Order of St Anna (3rd class) and the Order of St Vladimir (3rd class).

The photographs from these years portray a dashing and broad-shouldered officer adorned with medals, epaulettes, a sword and a well-groomed handlebar moustache. We see him with his cadet pupils, with a group of his comrades-in-arms, in his study, on training exercises, and on a walk with his wife.

The October Revolution of 1917 entirely changed the course of Levitsky's fortune. The Orlov Bakhtin Cadet Corps was closed and Levitsky, now serving the Soviet state, was appointed head of handicraft at Schools Numbers 1 and 3 in Oryol. He fought for the Reds in the Civil War, serving in the headquarters of the 12th Army on the Ukrainian front. In his own memoirs, Levitsky's son, Oleg, quotes extracts from his father's military service file, in which his commanding officer states that he

> possesses great resolve, decisiveness and discipline and has the necessary knowledge for commanding soldiers and carrying out both his administrative and military training duties. He is very precise, efficient and impartial, and treats his subordinates fairly and with respect. He is attentive to their needs and always ready to help them.

Following Levitsky's demobilisation, the family relocated to Natalya's hometown of Kursk. Here they moved back into her former family home, which by this time had been nationalised by the new Soviet state. To begin with, Levitsky worked as head of department at the Gubprodkom* before becoming a statistician at the Kursk branch of *Soyuzmyaso*, the agency responsible for meat production in the USSR. His was now the modest life of a humble Soviet civil servant.

When tragedy struck, it was from an unexpected direction. In the early 1930s the Soviet government had set out to crush all unofficial private sector organisations. The reason was obvious; not only was it difficult to control associations of volunteers, but their social composition was deemed to be of a 'dubious nature' and they did not fit comfortably into the newly constructed communist system. Not even the most outwardly respectable organisations, such as the Russian Association of Proletarian Writers, escaped the claws of repression. Many others such as the Society of Amateur Gardeners, the All-Union Poets' Union, the Society of Ex-Librists, Marxist-Historians, Friends of the Book, the Beethoven Society were also targeted.

One of the first societies to fall victim to the government's assault on unofficial organisations was the All-Russian Society of Stamp Collectors, of which Vladimir Levitsky had the misfortune to be an active member. Levitsky had founded the Society of Stamp Collectors back in 1925 and had since been chosen to stand as its president. His knowledge of French and German enabled him to correspond and exchange stamps with philatelists in Germany, Switzerland, France, Denmark, Holland and Latin America. This correspondence alone had already aroused the suspicion of the OGPU, particularly as the letters exchanged between the stamp collectors were peppered with confusing columns of numbers, which were naturally assumed to be encrypted messages. That the figures were merely stamp catalogue numbers was of little interest to the investigators.

In his memoirs Oleg Levitsky writes:

---

* The Provincial Food Committee.

In early January 1931 my father came home and told my mother that he had been summoned that afternoon to the OGPU (Number 6 Bebel Street) for a conversation of some sort. He seemed anxious. I was only fifteen years old at the time and didn't pay much attention, but my mother was worried. On 18 March we were awoken during the night by a knock at the door to our apartment. Two men entered: a Red Army soldier carrying a carbine, and his supervisor, a man half-dressed in army uniform who was later revealed to be Investigator Kotov. I don't remember whether there were any independent witnesses. Having presented some documents, Kotov set about searching the house . . . The search was soon over and Kotov told my mother that Father was to be held at the OGPU station for half an hour (it was very close to our house), and that he would then be returned home. My father took with him a folder containing the letters that he had exchanged with other stamp collectors, both in the USSR and abroad, as well as a catalogue of stamps and a few other papers. Then they left. Not for a moment did it cross our minds that Father had gone forever.

Levitsky was held in Kursk from 18 March 1931 until 3 August of that year. His granddaughter, Natalya Petrovanova, believes that he was interrogated, and probably beaten. In 2001 she was able to find out a little more about her grandfather's 'case' and noted that the interrogation records looked absolutely ludicrous. 'My grandfather confessed to all sorts of absurd "crimes"', she wrote, 'and gave the names of his fellow stamp collectors and "conspirators".' Ultimately, Levitsky was charged with 'participation in a counter-revolutionary officers' organisation' and sentenced to ten years' penal servitude in Siberia. Oleg writes:

The train left at night. Family members were gathered on the platform; many were crying. I walked up to the train carriage to give Father a teapot and some food supplies for the journey. He deliberately let the teapot fall so that I would pick it up and he could squeeze my hand. It was 12 August 1931.

Vladimir Levitsky's life in Siberia had its ups and downs. At first he was put to work in the camp's *komendatura** as a statistician on 'special resettlers' (dispossessed kulak peasants who had been sent to Siberia). This equated to life without an escort, trips on assignment, housing in the komendatura outside the camp precincts, a regular salary, tolerable food and other such privileges that were not extended to ordinary prisoners. He wrote the return address 'Gorno-Shorsky Komendatura for Special Resettlers, Myski, Kuznetsk, West-Siberia Region' on his letters. He writes:

I am now working and am a completely free citizen
aside from one restriction: I do not have the right to take
any leave. Other than that, I am entirely free. My work
involves recording and registering the new arrivals here.
(16.10.1931)

I still feel as though I am on assignment and am so
happy to be free that I have forgotten the past 8 months
of suffering. What a great joy it is to be free . . .
(17.11.1931)

We live in the apartment for prisoners not under close
police guard. [. . .] At least when you come home in
the evening, drink some tea and read a newspaper by

---

* The camp administrative office where prisoners were recorded and processed.

candlelight your soul can enjoy a break from people. We
go to bed at 9 or 10pm. (21.11.1931)

We are all registered as prisoners . . . they send us
to work and we carry out our duties. We have been
told that we are 90 per cent free; we do not have any
restrictions placed upon us, bar being denied the right
to leave our place of work. We do go on business trips
though, and our local department travels to Kuznetsk
and to Novosibirsk. [. . .] And so my position is neither
that of an administrative exile, nor a special resettler (of
dispossessed kulaks) but rather a person assigned to work
for the camp. What is more, my service will be offset by a
reduction in my sentence by ¼ . . . (11.01.1932)

Levitsky was able to subscribe to a newspaper, buy groceries at
the market and in local shops, send and receive unlimited letters
and parcels and even continue collecting his beloved stamps.
'Today is a stamp-collecting celebration day for me. I received
12 of the 1931 issues of the *The Soviet Collector* journal from
Novosibirsk,' Levitsky wrote to his son. 'It is a shame, Olyusha,
that we can't read them together . . .' (16.04.1932) Moreover,
the salary that he received enabled him to send money home in
addition to parcels. In terms of work, there was a lot to do, but
at least it was a familiar desk job. Indeed, he wrote in one letter
that his work at the camp was, 'exactly the same as my work for
the Central Meat Union'.

In letters home he asked his son to send issues of *The Soviet
Collector*, new stamps, drawings, and fountain pens for writing
letters. His letters are restrained in their depiction of his
emotional state.

I now work alone in a separate room. The next-door

room contains the red corner* and a radio . . . recently it played a piece of music – a waltz from the operetta 'Der Bettelstudent'. I remember going to this operetta with your mother in St Petersburg and on hearing the music I began to cry (I was alone in the room). But this happened just the once; I feel good the rest of the time when I am around people and busy with work. (09.02.1932)

Levitsky sent his son drawings, stamps and books, hoping to instil in him an interest in collecting.

Olyusha! I am sending you a book for your library along with this letter. Collect a few books – having even a small personal library will bring you great pleasure. I am also sending you 'bookplates' for your little library. (20.04.1932)

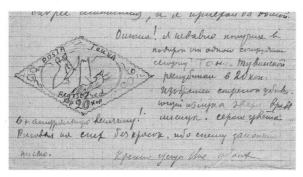

'Olyusha! I recently received this present from a colleague – a 20-kopek stamp from the Tuvan People's Republic. It depicts a grey animal resembling a fox being shot by an arrow fired from a bow. I have drawn it to scale, hurriedly, and without colours . . .' Olkhovka, 30.03.1934

In July 1932, Levitsky was sent 1,000 kilometres further east, to the command headquarters in the Olkhovsky district.

---

* Traditionally a sacred corner of a room or house decorated with religious icons. During Soviet times, the red corner became a place glorifying the party or state leaders; portraits of Lenin or Stalin or propagandist posters were often hung in place of religious icons.

The majority of the prisoners in this labour camp worked in the local gold mines, but here, as in Myski, Levitsky had the good fortune to be put in charge of records. He was also permitted to live outside the mine precincts, sharing a room at the command headquarters, at first with two men, and latterly just one. He became a member of the library and began to read voraciously and admire the classics that he had not yet read. He devoured Leo Tolstoy, Ivan Goncharov, Mikhail Saltykov-Shchedrin and Nikolai Leskov, and gave the following advice to his wife and son:

> Natasha and Olyusha! Read this short story (Leskov's 'Lefty'). Olyusha! Get hold of it and read it aloud to your mother. I was in such raptures when I read it. (06.08.1933)

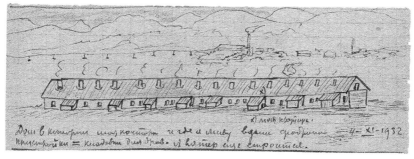

'The building that houses my office, and in which I also live. The factory is in the distance and the little extensions are stores for firewood. The lavatory is still under construction.' Olkhovka, 04.11.1932.

The work conditions and daily life in Olkhovka were just as they had been in Kuznetsk, but Levitsky's financial situation deteriorated. He was no longer able to send parcels and money home and needed to make concessions himself.

> For lunch yesterday I had: soup (35 kopeks) + fish (55 kopeks) + a meat patty (1 rouble, 10 kopeks) = 2 roubles in total. I didn't have dessert – there was jelly for 70 kopeks, but I do not spend more than 2 roubles per day. (06.08.1933)

'My study'; a drawing of Levitsky's office, Olkhovka, 1933.

He could endure the lack of food, but the heavy burden of his sorrow at having been wrenched away from home became harder and harder to bear.

> Natasha! Write and tell me whether Olyusha remembers me? I, who have been torn away from my family. Olyusha! There are just three things that grieve me. The first is that I don't see you or your mother. The second – I don't have my stamp albums, and the third – I am experiencing a terrible and frightening sense of outrage at the injustice of it all . . . (03.11.1932)

> If somebody had foretold all that would befall my family, I would not have believed them. Olyusha! Be compassionate towards your mother – do not upset her. She has suffered a lot and is saintlike to me now. (12.11.1932)

> Olyusha, go out into the courtyard one evening on a

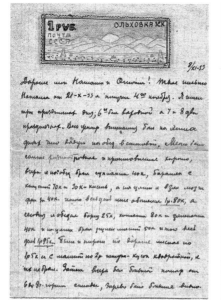

A letter with hand-drawn stamp,
Olkhovka, 21.11.1933.

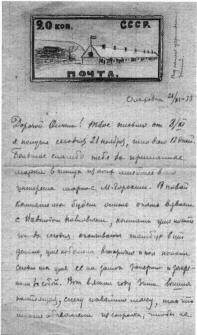

A letter with hand-drawn stamp,
Olkhovka, 08.11.1933.

A handmade envelope.

starry night and look up at the Big Bear. Imagine that I
too am looking at it right at that minute and our gaze will
meet up in the stars. This will make things easier for me.
(12.05.1933)

Vladimir Levitsky turned sixty at Olkhovka. In another letter home he wrote:

> Damn all those people who have wronged me, an innocent man, so terribly. Over the last two years I have learnt so much, seen so many people, so much grief, sadness, injustice, truth and a greater truth, that I now know and understand it all. I can now say for certain that it is not I who has been punished, but my family, who have had to endure so much suffering. (27.07.1933)

A drawing of Artemovsk mining camp in winter, Olkhovka, 1933.

Baskets of ore, Artemovsk mine, Olkhovka, 1933.

Levitsky, like so many of his fellow prisoners, hoped that his case would be reviewed. He wrote a letter to the prosecutor's office, petitioned the Gulag directors when they visited his camp and awaited amnesty . . .

He also placed high hopes in a 'Gulag Commission' that was due to arrive from Moscow in October 1933, and wrote to tell his family that, 'our managers are seeking educated people to take over the current prisoners' jobs . . . and we are all to be replaced.' (01.10.1933) It appears that Levitsky and his comrades somewhat naively saw in this substitution an opportunity for freedom: 'It is possible that those who filed a request for their case to be reviewed will be released,' he wrote.

As it transpired, events unfolded in the opposite way. The Gulag directors hired free labourers to perform the desk jobs, and the prisoners who had previously occupied these roles were dispatched to where they were deemed to belong: on the other side of the barbed wire. Levitsky was sent to Mariinsk.

One might say that here too he was lucky, for he was appointed as record manager in the camp hospital. By this time, however, he was sleeping on a hard plank bunk in a barracks with sixty other men and contending with bed bugs, filth and watery gruel: 'Soup or borscht – just a beetroot in water – and dinner and breakfast consist of porridge, 2 little fish per person and 600 grams of rye bread per day.' (15.05.1934)

Feelings of depression, intense sorrow and a sense of hopelessness returned with an even greater vengeance, and his letters began to reference suicidal despair.

> . . . it is some sort of apathy; a sense of meaninglessness which weighs heavily on the soul. Thoughts of you, my darlings, are all that sustain me; if it weren't for you, I would no longer be here. (15.05.1934)

There were no longer any tales about his daily life (heaven

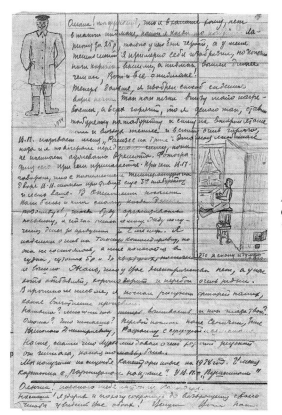

A letter from Levitsky to Oleg, Olkhovka, 7 January 1934.

'Olyusha! This is the place on the River Mrass where I swim every day. The river is 200 steps wide. The steep bank is in blue. I'm in the picture. This is where I get undressed. Clothes and slippers.'

forbid they should come to the attention of the camp censorship authorities), and the miniature watercolours that he sent home to his son depicted landscapes from his former life – the sea, Livadia,* a sunset, a moonlit night . . .

> There is so much more to write, but it would be better
> if I were to tell you myself when we meet. No books
> can adequately describe what a man sees and experiences
> during his time in a camp – there is much to tell. Olyusha!
> In line with the camp's censorship rules I won't send
> you any drawings from here so as to spare myself any
> unpleasantness. (16.06.1934)

> My life's goal is to see you again and return home
> (08.11.1934)

Levitsky's every thought revolved around his release; about the possibility of receiving amnesty in time for the celebration of the anniversary of the October Revolution; after another meeting of the All-Russian Central Executive Committee (VTSIK); after the adoption of the [Stalin] Constitution . . .

> One thought alone occupies all of our minds. We
> discuss and look forward to it, and it is with this thought
> alone that we fall asleep at night and wake up in the
> morning . . . (30.06.1936)

Deep down in his soul he recognised the fallacy of this hope and increasingly, he placed his trust in God.

> I pray to God, asking only that he give me the strength

---

* Livadia is a small village on the Crimean south coast and home to the Livadia Palace, a summer residence of the Russian tsars.

and health to survive until the moment that I am told I
am free and can return home. (11.03.1935)

I have already quite ceased to laugh and smile when
others do so. My entire mindset has altered radically and I
am now a completely different man from the cheery and
upbeat person I once was. I don't think that I will even
talk to anybody other than you two when I return home.
I am so fed up with people that becoming a hermit would
bring me great pleasure. (05.04.1936)

It must be noted that while he was fully aware of the reality
of the injustice that had been served to him, Levitsky's letters
never contained even the slightest hint of remonstrance against
the authorities. Although this can partly be attributed to a
fear of camp censorship, it is worth noting that Levitsky had
been trained to conform to the military custom of submission
to one's superiors. He believed that life on the outside was
taking a rational and appropriate course and maintained his

Postcard by V. Levitsky, Mariinsk, 1935.

unfaltering dedication to social activism and hard work even while incarcerated in the Gulag.

> Olyusha! Has the Stakhanovite movement reached you? Here with us it is in full swing. The best workers can earn a reduction in their sentence and better food. A five day 'Stakhanov period' is underway here at the moment, and I am putting forward a proposal . . . (28.01.1935)

On learning that his son had begun work, Levitsky wrote to him:

> I am so pleased to hear that you are on the right track and that your superiors value your qualities and are promoting you. Cherish this opportunity, and do not botch it – you do not want to forfeit their trust. (14.03.1935)

Had this loyal, conscientious and kind-hearted man not fallen under the oppressive weight of repression, he would doubtless have lived out his life as an ordinary Soviet citizen, a diligent worker and a loving family man with a passion for stamp collecting.

Vladimir Levitsky was sentenced to death by an NKVD troika in the Novosibirsk Region on 8 December 1937. He was shot on 20 December

Photo of Vladimir Levitsky taken from his case file, 1937.

alongside twenty other prisoners from the Suslovo branch of the Siblag,* to where he had been transferred from Mariinsk at the end of 1936.

---

* Siberian Labour Camp

Envelope containing a letter addressed to V. Levitsky in 1937. The letter was returned to its sender with a note in pencil stating that the addressee had 'departed'.

Vladimir Levitsky's son Oleg (1915–2002) fought in the front line during the Great Patriotic War and later became an architect. He was a well-known local historian in Oryol and pieced together the history of the Orlov Bakhtin Cadet Corps where his father had worked. He inherited his father's love of stamp collecting and preserved and added to his collection.

Vladimir's son, Oleg Levitsky, Kursk, late 1930s.

Levitsky's wife, Natalia Nikolaevna, did not live to see her husband rehabilitated. She died in 1950.

Friedrich Krause

'. . . not to disappear completely from the face of the Earth . . .'

The following lines are taken from the autobiography of Friedrich Krause (1887–1973):

> My soul searches for a connection between past and present, between present and future [. . .] I have a strong desire not to disappear completely from the face of the Earth, along with my complex and precious innermost thoughts and experiences. I want to hand them on . . . to those who will follow after us.

Friedrich Krause began to write his memoirs at the height of the Russian Civil War, aged just twenty-three. On the cover of the first of the notebooks containing his recollections is written: 'To my daughter, when she grows up. Notes and Thoughts. 1919'. At the time of writing, his daughter from his first marriage, Irina, was only two years old.

Friedrich Krause, June, 1973

Krause's second wife later gave birth to another daughter, Elena, in 1929, followed by a son, Oscar, in 1932. He continued to write his memoirs between

175

Friedrich Krause with his daughter,
Elena, Magnitogorsk, 1932.

1950 and 1970, following his release from a labour camp, but unfortunately he never managed to complete them.

Friedrich was born into a family of 'Russian Germans' who, though they identified as members of the Russian community and spoke both Russian and German fluently, chose to uphold and celebrate certain German traditions. His father, a Baltic German, had arrived in Moscow in 1880 and taken up a teaching position at the Mikhailovsky Realschule. Krause left home early, graduating from the Medical Faculty at Moscow University before starting work in 1912 as a paediatrician in the Morozovsky Children's Hospital. When the First World War broke out in 1914, he became an army doctor. Krause embraced the February revolution of 1917 and accepted the subsequent Soviet accession to power without protest, considering it an inevitable matter of course. He spent two years of the Civil War (1918–1920) working as chief physician in the large 39th Emergency Field Hospital, criss-crossing through the governorates of Central Russia, which were at that time in the grip of an epidemic of typhoid and Spanish influenza. At the end of 1919, the hospital moved to the city of Ufa, approximately 1,300 kilometres south-east of Moscow, taking him with it.

Krause continued to practise medicine in Ufa and before long he succeeded in establishing a separate children's branch of the city hospital. It was to be the first children's hospital in the city, and he essentially founded it from scratch. His first wife, Alexandra Dobrohotova, was also a paediatrician, and shortly after Krause arrived in Ufa, she and her daughter, Irina, left the cold and hunger of Moscow to join him. Here too the family had much to contend with: the bitter cold, a smoky cast-iron stove, scanty food rations, not to mention a young child. Nevertheless, they categorically refused to entertain the notion of emigration.

Krause and his wife shared a domestic and professional life from 1916 until they separated in 1928. Alexandra was a talented doctor in her own right and an eminent specialist in infectious diseases in children. She was later to become an Associate Fellow of the USSR's Academy of Medical Science.

In his memoirs, written for his daughter, Krause says:

> I remember the scepticism and mocking smiles with which the elderly local doctors decried our plans. 'They have undertaken a venture to establish a children's hospital! Soviet nonsense!' they said. 'And what mother is going to entrust her child to you? Absolutely nothing will come of this!' [. . .] There were two camps of thought: those who accepted the new system, and those who did not.
>
> In general, those who rejected the new state of affairs were the respected and established local doctors who had been raised on, and grown used to, many years of private practice, without which they couldn't conceive of practising medicine. [. . .] They predicted that our 'little venture' with the children's hospital was doomed to fail. What poor prophets they were! [. . .] On the whole, we were optimistic back then. Many people tolerantly endured the hardships, for we believed in a brighter future, and worked hard to achieve it. [. . .] Naturally, there were no ill wishers and nobody gloated over our failures and, more importantly, there was no sabotage, incidences of which were prevalent among the intelligentsia at that time. I clearly remember our conversations about not only the bourgeoisie fleeing

across the border, but also a fair number of frightened members of the intelligentsia. We didn't understand them and condemned them harshly for their lack of faith in their people. We considered them moral pariahs for their decision to sever themselves from the land of their birth.

Friedrich Krause was by no means a romantic, nor did he look at the world through rose-tinted glasses. The young doctor could see for himself the deficit in qualifications and lack of culture in the ignorant and opportunistic newly appointed heads of hospital departments. And yet, despite being confronted with this reality, he maintained a deep and almost messianic conviction in his life's purpose. In a letter to his daughter in the 1920s he wrote:

> In the vast majority of cases, the people running our
> outfit are completely unfamiliar with the matters to which
> they have been assigned and they are in no way prepared
> for the administrative side of affairs. But there are also a
> significant number of people who are purely pernicious;
> they are little kings whose interests lie above all in their
> own well-being. These people don't give a damn about
> the needs of the community, far less the needs of the
> government. They do not understand what is required,
> and, what's more, they do not want to understand,
> despite all their fancy phraseology. It is all for the sake of
> appearances. It is very, very difficult to get something up
> and running under these circumstances . . . Of course,
> my position remains unchanged: I am grateful for fate,
> which has given me the opportunity to become a doctor
> and put me in this position at such an historic moment;
> at a difficult time that demands compromise from many.
> Mine is a position that does not require me to make
> compromises on matters of my conscience at all. It does,

however, allow me to strive for and to carry out work that is purely cultural, formative and essential in every way.

In Krause's memoirs addressed to his daughter he writes:

When Irinochka reads this notebook (provided that she does read it), she will be surprised. How can it be that Mama and Papa lived through such a fascinating period in history; the age of revolution, a revolution with objectives and a scale so grandiose that even the great French Revolution barely compares with it, and yet in their correspondence, even in Papa's diary, they recount just the same ordinary old things: personal experiences, family heartache, concerns about how best to endure the hunger and the cold, and all sorts of other trivial matters. There is almost no mention at all of the greatness being accomplished all around, about the powerful forces and tempests that future generations will study, envying those 'lucky ones' whose fate it was to be sucked into the whirlwind's vortex, and to be crushed beneath its might.

His words might be construed as a little bombastic, but there can be no denying their sincerity and, more importantly, their prescience.

In 1921, Krause and his family moved to Moscow, where he began work at the Losinoostrovsky Sanatorium. Here he was tasked with running the Department of Maternal and Infant Health, and it was at this same hospital that he met his second wife, Vera

Friedrich Krause and Vera Bersenyova, Magnitogorsk, 1939.

Bersenyova. They married in 1928 and in 1930 Vera gave birth to a daughter, Elena, followed by a son, Oscar, in 1932. (Oscar is affectionately referred to as 'Karik' in many of the letters.) By the time Oscar was born, Krause and Vera had moved to the new industrial city of Magnitogorsk, in the southern Urals. Krause soon became the city's leading paediatrician and earned the well-founded respect of both his colleagues and patients' parents.

Up until the outbreak of the Second World War, Krause's life could not have been better. However, as the war gathered momentum, he began to sense that:

> . . . the local Ministry of Internal Affairs was watching me, and this meant that I was next in line . . . and yet nevertheless I foolishly placed hope in our spotless reputation and the total absence of any sort of incriminating evidence. And so we went on living our ordinary lives, albeit with a few tremors of anxiety within our hearts. We had nothing to hide, and covered nothing up.

His hopes were in vain. They came for him on 10 March 1942, and his wife was arrested later the same year, on 4 December. At the time of their arrests, their children, Lena (Elena) and Karik (Oscar), were just twelve and ten years old respectively.

Both Vera and Krause's first wife, Alexandra, were women of exceptional moral standards and when Vera was sent to a labour camp in the wake of her husband's arrest in 1942, Alexandra stepped in, without hesitation, to look after her children. Elena moved into her house and remembers 'Auntie Sasha'* with great love and affection.

Vera was a 'Bestuzhevka',† spoke several foreign languages and

---

* Sasha is a diminutive form of the name Alexandra in Russian.
† The name given to graduates of the prestigious Bestuzhev Courses in St Petersburg, the first higher education institution for women in Russia (1878–1918).

was a very eloquent writer (her letters could serve as exemplary models of the epistolary genre). She continued to write about her love for Friedrich Krause up until the very final moments of her life. Below he writes to Vera:

> My poor, poor unfortunate wife. Intertwining my fate
> with yours has not brought you joy! Not for a minute
> did I imagine that our happy marriage would meet such
> a dismal end. [. . .] If we die before we see each other
> again, at least we will know until the very end that each
> of us, with our last breath, was blessing the other and
> remembering the happiness of the past . . . my darling!

This was the beginning of the 'camp to camp' correspondence between husband and wife. It had taken Krause thirteen months to track Vera down, and his joy at finding her alive was marred by the discovery that she too had been arrested and imprisoned in a labour camp thousands of kilometres from his own. He was shaken to his very soul, not only by her arrest, but also by the collapse of his family and the now parentless state of his children. Vera wrote to Krause:

> Even had I been forewarned of all the adversity that
> fate would deal us, I would not have denied myself the
> happiness of being your wife.

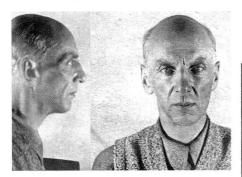

Prison photographs of Friedrich Krause and Vera Bersenyova, 1942.

In an extract from Friedrich Krause's memoirs, written in 1970, he says:

> I was asked to put down in writing my relationship to the Soviet State. And I wrote absolutely truthfully that in conversations at home I had criticised the haste with which the policy of collectivisation had been implemented across the entire nation in one great sweep. I wrote that I considered the difficult Winter War with Finland a mistake because it alienated such a wide set of foreign workers, who were otherwise sympathetic to our cause. I also wrote that I was pained by the recent abolition of student grants in secondary medical schools, which had forced many of the best students to abandon their education. But I vehemently (and this is also true) denied engaging in any sort of 'agitation', or anything at odds with our constitutional guarantees.

His interrogation lasted for days and nights on end. The interrogators did not allow Krause to sleep and demanded that he testify against colleagues. Krause remembered that he twice came within an inch of committing suicide. But he held on, and didn't name a single person. He was sentenced to death, but a little later this sentence was commuted to ten years in a corrective labour camp.

He would probably have died from disease and exhaustion had he not been unexpectedly transferred from the Karlag (Karaganda Corrective Labour Camp) to a different camp near the city of Mary.* There he worked in the camp medical wing, supervising the Children's House.† He was a strong-willed

---

* Today this city is in Turkmenistan.
† Children's houses were established in several corrective labour facilities to house the children born in the camp. Imprisoned women were allowed to breastfeed their newborns (and in some cases also allowed to live with them), visit them and spend brief spells of time with them. Once children reached the age of three, they were either sent to state-run orphanages or sent away to be

man, and tried hard to do more than simply survive. He set himself a task: he would not succumb to either moral or mental degradation, and would resist the effects of the surrounding camp environment with all his strength and willpower. Below are extracts from his letters to Vera:

> Morally speaking, the most awful thing of all is finding oneself among people who share the moral standards of the types of people one would find in a brothel. On the gloomiest days in Kazakhstan I have occasionally managed to get hold of some sort of book or newspaper, and these have saved me from the moral filth that surrounds me . . .

> I have not, and will not, become a typical 'camp inmate', with a mind that is degenerating alongside both physical and moral deterioration. Aside from the skills that I acquired in childhood, I have been saved by my ability to occupy my mind intellectually, which has meant that I cannot get bored. [. . .] Over the past few years, I have often suffered from deep sorrow, but never boredom. At first, I taught anatomy, physiology, nutritional science, infectious diseases and language (for a few hours every day over several months). I taught myself French and Accountancy, and discussed things I read with others. Wherever possible, I tried to get hold of books [. . .] Ultimately, my soul has been much enriched by thoughts of infinite possibilities, both in hindsight and in terms of our own, and our children's, future. [. . .] Don't worry, I won't disgrace my family with faint-heartedness or fruitless scepticism.

---

brought up by relatives.

In letters to his children he says:

> In my sleep I constantly see books; I see myself ferreting
> around in second-hand bookshops. [. . .] Take good care
> of everything we still have, especially any family memoirs,
> letters, drawings, photos and so on. Be good, and by
> that I mean you should always be honest, brave and kind
> comrades. Demonstrate your love for your homeland
> through hard work and action, and not with words alone.
> But never limit yourselves to national boundaries – you
> absolutely must study foreign languages and cultures to
> broaden your intellectual horizons. Most importantly, you
> must study and study, to accrue knowledge while you
> are young. [. . .] Collect and look after things of cultural
> value – books, sheet music and vinyl records. (Karlag
> 12.01.1944)

> To you I am somewhere behind the clouds, out of sight
> and beyond reach. I cannot actively partake in your lives
> with either words or deeds. Nor can I give you advice or
> help, and coming to terms with this is very, very difficult
> for me. But do you both still remember the winter of
> 1941/42, when we sat on the sofa and read Irving's
> 'Legend'* and 'Don Quixote'? Oh, how wonderful
> that was. And surely you will never be able to forget
> our family life, so happy and complete. We so enjoyed
> listening to good music together – remember how hard
> we would try to get hold of the best vinyl records and
> books! [. . .] Oh, how I always dreamed that I would
> give my children the best education and provide them
> with the world's literary and musical treasures . . . (Mary,
> 11.07.1945)

★ *The Legend of Sleepy Hollow* by Washington Irving.

My darling daughter, sweet Lenusha. Over the last few days I have received two of your airmail postcards, from the 5th and the 7th; they arrived after your letter. So it appears that our connection has been restored. Thank you for your little letters; they brought me so much joy. I now know at last that you have finished school and are already thinking about higher education. It is true that until you mentioned Chemistry, I had my doubts. I thought that perhaps you were sitting your mid-term tests, which you wrote and told me you had an awful lot of. But I now realise that you were not talking about mid-term tests, but your final exams. At last! At least that weight has now been lifted from your shoulders. And you passed them well, perhaps even with a medal. So all roads will be open to you and you can take whichever one you choose . . . I am of course surprised that you have not gone down the humanities route, but it doesn't upset me in the least. I myself am a doctor, but you know how varied my interests are. And this really, truly brightens life up. I am absolutely certain that no matter where their specialities lie, my children will also have broad horizons and diverse multicultural interests – in a word, they will not be one-sided like a gumboil. Karik has obviously finished his exams. I hope to receive a letter from him too, even just a short note about his exams and plans for the summer. It would be interesting to know whether he enjoyed the books I sent. I intend to send Lermontov* and something else. You have probably also received 'Sevastopol Harvest'† by now. Will you have time to read it? Or have you already read it? The only thing that upsets me is that you still want to send me some things . . . but heaven knows I need nothing here, nothing other than books,

---

* Mikhail Lermontov was a leading Russian Romantic poet and writer.

† *Sevastopol Harvest* (*Sevastopolskaya Strada*) is a book by Sergei Sergeev Tsensky.

that is. Well, goodbye for now. I'm sending you a kiss and
a hug. Your loving Papa (Mary. 15.06.1949)

Thank you, my darling daughter, for sending me your
postcards so often and for letting me know how you
got on in your exams. It is just a shame that you did not
mention your grades – you probably don't know them
yourself yet. I dream about you achieving a medal all
the time – it will make it easy for you to get into any
university. Study Chemistry then if you like! It is by
no means bad if you fall in love with this subject and
do well in it. Only, where are you thinking of applying
to? A university? The Mendeleev Institute? Or some
other specialist technical training college? Chemistry is
useful everywhere, both in practice and in scientific and

Letter from Friedrich Krause to Lena showing
lines crossed out by camp censorship, 21 June
1949.

industrial laboratories. There are all sorts of paths leading from it and many corresponding threads. My dear, once you have sat your final exam and have had a little time to relax, you must write me a detailed letter telling me about your plans, answering my questions (since I haven't received an answer for several years!) and informing me about the family mementos (Ruf's schoolboy poems, your drawings, exercise books, first letters, photos). I will hope . . . [the following lines were crossed out by camp censorship]. I wish you good health and courage. How are you after your heartbreak? Write and tell me everything. I am sending you a big kiss, my sweet daughter. Papa.

P.S. I wrote a letter to Karik 4 days ago (Mary. 21.06.1949)

Vera died in a labour camp near Mariinsk (Kemerovo region) on 1 August 1950. By then, Krause had only a year and a half to wait before his scheduled release. He considered the death of his wife to be the greatest catastrophe of his life, and it shattered all of his hopes for the future. He served the full length of his ten-year prison sentence from start to finish – he was incarcerated from 10 March 1942 until 10 March 1952. According to his son, he returned from the camp a faded, broken man; a barely recognisable shadow of his former self.

He moved to the Vologodchina region to work as a children's doctor, deep in a remote forest district inhabited by peaceful and kind-hearted Russian people, among silence, water and trees. What delighted him most was the wonderful bookshop he found there, which received all the latest publications. For the first three years following his release, Krause was inundated with work. He quickly regained his former energy and professional form, and got the regional children's hospital back up and running to exemplary standards. Here too, Krause's medical talent and meticulous scruples won him the hearts of colleagues and patients alike, and he was still remembered fondly by them many years later.

Krause retired in the autumn of 1956, aged sixty-nine, and moved to the Oryol region of Russia where he could be closer to his Moscow-based daughters. He was fully rehabilitated in 1962 and spent the final years of his life in the little old town of Bolkhov, where he tended his fruit garden. He visited his daughters in Moscow, travelled to his beloved Magnitogorsk a couple of times, met with friends and worked on his memoirs. He died in 1973, three days before his eighty-sixth birthday.

Friedrich Krause's eldest daughter, Irina, earned two degrees, first graduating from the Moscow Institute of Foreign Languages, before adding a medical degree to her name. She worked as a paediatric doctor and taught French alongside her medical work until her death in 1993.

Krause and Vera's children were equally successful: Oscar graduated from the 2nd Moscow Institute of Medicine and followed in his father's footsteps, becoming a distinguished children's surgeon. He founded a hospital specialising in children's surgery in Cherepovets and was nominated an honorary citizen of the city. He also collated and published a book about his mother, Vera Bersenyova, which contained extracts from his parents' camp correspondence. Oscar's sister, Elena, became an automotive engineer and enjoyed a successful career in car manufacturing. She worked for many years in the USSR Car Manufacturing Ministry for Food and Light Industries.

Samuil Tieits

'The picture of my father conjured up by my memory . . .'

This chapter is taken from the memoirs of Nina Tieits.

My father, Samuil Tieits, was born in Warsaw in June 1895. His father was a travelling salesman who roamed from city to city, both in Russia and abroad, peddling samples of ironware and hardware. His mother, in trying to have

Samuil Tieits, 1920.

a daughter, had given birth to six sons in quick succession and Samuil (Mulek in Polish) arrived eighteen months after the first son, David. When my father turned six, he was enrolled at the cheder* where his elder brother David was already a pupil. He then went on to receive his formal primary education at the local gymnasium from 1905 to 1914, studying on a full bursary for almost eight years, as his family did not possess the means to pay for his education. As soon as they were able, both David and Samuil began tutoring to earn a living.

On finishing school in 1914, my father was very fortunate to gain a place in the Medical Faculty at the University of Warsaw. I say very fortunate because at that time only five per cent of

---

* A religious elementary school teaching the basics of Judaism and the Hebrew language.

university places were allocated to Jews, and by a sheer stroke of serendipity he drew a lucky number during the admissions process. The First World War struck shortly afterwards and he put his medical training into practice as a hospital attendant in small Red Cross hospitals and medical facilities in Warsaw. When German and Austro-Hungarian soldiers occupied Russian territory in Poland, the Tieits family evacuated to Moscow. Warsaw University was relocated to Rostov-on-Don and in 1915 my father moved there in order to continue his studies at the Medical Faculty. Meanwhile, he also resumed his work as a hospital attendant in a Red Cross hospital.

When the Rostov workers formed a Red Guard force in August 1917, my father helped to prepare and educate the Red Guard medical division, and in November 1917 he was nominated as head of the medical division responsible for the combat regions of Rostov-on-Don, Nakhichevan and Bataysk. When the Whites captured Rostov, he and the remaining Red Guards left the city. He returned a short while later alongside a few Red Guard divisions and, once again, picked up his

Samuil Tieits, Warsaw, 1914.   Samuil and Cecilia Tieits, 1919.

university studies and resumed his work as a doctor in the Red Cross infirmary. When at last he completed his fourth year in the medical division, my father left Rostov for Moscow. He enrolled to complete the final year of his medical education at Moscow State University's Medical Faculty, from where he graduated in February 1919. Throughout his final year he juggled his studies alongside a position as deputy head of the Raizdrav (the Regional Public Health Care Administration) in the Zamoskvorechye District.

In April 1919, my father married the woman who was to become my mother: Cecilia Aruin. My mother had also studied medicine, and, like my father, she had graduated from the Medical Faculty at Warsaw University. Her specialism, however, was dentistry. They had met a few years earlier, in 1916, and had kept up a near-constant correspondence despite the fact that my father's role as an army doctor meant that he was regularly on the move with the Red Guards. Over the course of two and a half years, he spent time in the south-west, in Arkhangelsk and on both the western and southern fronts. Having begun his career as a junior regimental doctor, by the time he had completed his service he was head of the Medical Division of the Ukrainian Workers' Army. He was a member of the Kharkov City Soviet from 1920 to 1921 and it was there in Kharkov that I was born in 1920, his one and only beloved daughter.

In August 1921, my father left Kharkov to take part in a doctor's development programme at Moscow State University. While there, he taught several courses at the vocational *profshkola*.* Between 1923 and 1936 he was the senior medical inspector on the Moscow committee of the Metalworkers'

---

* A school where vocational skills were taught alongside traditional subjects. Translator's note: The *profshkola* was advertised as a high-minded rejection of that 'creation of bourgeois government', the academic secondary school. (Shelia Fitzpatrick, *Education and Social Mobility in the Soviet Union 1921–1934* (Cambridge University Press, 1979), p.46.

Union and for much of this time (1925 to 1930) he also ran the Simonovsky Outpatient Association (a group of district clinics which served the Dinamo, AMO and Parostroy factories among others). As a specialist in the field of sanitary working conditions within the manufacturing industry, he was regularly asked to report the findings of his work at the All-Union Congresses of Hygiene Experts in Hungary and Germany.

I remember one particular episode of my father's life from this period especially well. When returning from one of his international hygiene conferences, via Poland, he broke his journey in Warsaw and paid a visit to all the places associated with his favourite childhood memories. While there, he happened upon a male beauty contest. Out of curiosity, he entered . . . and won a prize! The award itself was a jumper, which at home we all called 'To Beauty!'. Evidently my father was deemed to have satisfied all the necessary criteria for male beauty.

In July 1929 my father decided to devote himself entirely to the study of science, and he won a place to study at the Obukh Institute for Workplace Safety. In 1932 he became a senior lecturer in hygiene in the workplace at the State Advanced Training Institute for Doctors and by 1935 he had graduated from the Moscow University of Marxism-Leninism with the title of 'Red Professor'. Meanwhile, he also gained a postgraduate degree in medical sciences at the State Advanced Training Institute for Doctors, based on his previously published work.

In 1936 he became head of the USSR Narkomzdrav* Department of Industrial Health for the All-Union State Health Inspectors, a position equivalent to Deputy People's Commissar.

The picture of my father conjured up by my memory is one of a brown-haired man with a dark complexion that tanned easily. He was tall and well built, with an intelligent face and a

---

* People's Commissariat of Public Health.

small moustache. His light Polish accent and manners of speech particular to the Polish intelligentsia stayed with him long after he left Warsaw. My father was polite to absolutely everybody, regardless of rank, and he was always the first to greet his acquaintances, doffing his hat or kissing a woman on the hand. He was sociable and level-headed, and I do not remember him ever being angry or raising his voice. I recall liking the way he listened to the people he talked to, asking them about their lives and offering advice. He had a wonderful sense of humour and would joke with a completely straight face, so it was often very difficult to work out whether or not he was saying something in jest. An avid reader, he had a particular fondness for Russian literature, in which he was very well versed. He spoke fluent Polish and German and also knew Yiddish, although I never heard him use the latter in conversation.

From early 1919, the Tieits family, including my grandmother, grandfather and father's brothers, had been living in a huge six-roomed apartment on Moscow's Petrovsky Lane. It was to this house that my father took his new wife, and it was here too that I grew up. My father was well established by this time and earning a good wage (700 roubles from the Advanced Training Institute for Doctors and 1,000 roubles for his responsibilities as Senior Medical Inspector) in addition to enjoying a whole host of other privileges. The family employed several domestic staff and my father played absolutely no part in household affairs; not once did I see him set foot in

The Tieits family in the courtyard outside their house on Petrovsky Lane, 1924.

the kitchen! His fortunate position meant that he could even afford to pop in the popular Einem confectioners on Petrovka Street once in a while to buy a box of expensive chocolates!

My childhood and adolescence passed in an atmosphere of endless parental love and amid all the opportunities and pleasantries that my father's position afforded our family. They were joyful, idyllic years, free from troubles of any kind. Later, having made it through the worst of the difficulties and tragic events, a few lines of Alexander Kushner's poetry resonated deep within my heart:

> Reading Nabokov, I thought about the fact
> That too happy a childhood is dangerous . . .

1936 was the last happy year. Until then, my father's brothers had also been on the rise. David was a member of the All-Union Communist Party (Bolsheviks) and the director of the Kremlin Central Health Clinic and Sanatorium. That year he went on a special assignment to France, accompanying an important medical specialist who had previously been a private physician to Stalin. Max, a graduate of Moscow State Technical University, was the manager of an aeroplane laboratory at the Central Aero Hydrodynamic Institute. He was awarded the Order of Lenin and presented with a GAZ-M1 car for his contribution to the first Polar route flight. This project, co-orchestrated by the celebrated Soviet pilots Valery Chkalov, Georgy Baidukov and Alexander Belyakov, entailed flying non-stop from Moscow to Vancouver via the North Pole in a single-engine plane.

The first alarm bell sounded in the summer of 1936 while we were on holiday in Kislovodsk. My father had been spending some time with Maxim Litvinov, the People's Commissar of Foreign Affairs, his deputy Lev Karakhan (shot in 1937) and Grigory Kaminsky, People's Commissar of Health (also shot in 1937). It was while we were in Kislovodsk that my father made a call to Moscow and learned that his brother, David, had been arrested. Not long afterwards, it was my father's turn.

The evening of 26 February 1938 remains engraved in my memory. Returning home from the institute (I had been studying at Moscow Medical Institute No. 1 since 1937), I noticed that several men of a 'specific type', but dressed in plain clothes, were walking up and down near the main entrance to our building. By now this was not unusual – there had been a flurry of arrests in our building and the presence of these men did not arouse particular worry in me. It was a chilly day, and large wet snowflakes were falling from the sky. Father returned home late, announcing, 'Happy is he who is home' as he came through the door. This phrase has stayed with me all my life.

That night, we were awoken by the sharp ring of the doorbell accompanied by loud banging on the door. Four men stood in the doorway: our caretaker, Nikolai, accompanied by two men dressed in plain clothes and one in military uniform. The officer presented the search and arrest warrant, which had been signed by Leonid Zakovsky, Deputy People's Commissar of the NKVD (who was shot at the end of 1938).

We were ordered to sit and told not to move or speak. The search lasted almost all night. Naturally, they found nothing incriminating, but they nevertheless gathered up a few photographs, letters and scientific manuscripts. My father communicated to me with his eyes that we needed to hide his letter to the procurator fiscal on the subject of workforce safety in industry (he believed this to be the reason for his arrest). I succeeded in hiding the letter and by the time morning came and he was taken away, my father had managed to sign a document giving my mother power of attorney, thereby enabling her to receive money in his absence.

I was astonished by my father's composure and self-control on the night of his arrest. Even after an exhausting search, nothing slipped his mind and his first thoughts were for his family who were, to all intents and purposes, being left without any means by which to survive. At the time of his arrest, he was supporting not only his wife who worked part-time as a dentist, but also myself and my husband, as we were both students, his pensionless mother, and the young daughter of his brother David, who had been arrested. (David's wife was arrested soon after my father.)

The time came for our indescribable, tragic and terrible farewell. Papa remained calm and composed and as he was led away, he said, 'It's a misunderstanding. They will sort it out and I'll be back soon.'

I never saw him again. He was just forty-two years old. I adored him, and we shared an exceptionally close bond; I was even closer to him than I was to my mother.

My father spent some time in the cells of the Lubyanka, before being transferred to Taganskaya Prison. There, he shared a single cell with one hundred and fifty men. There was little to no ventilation, and they received almost nothing to eat. There was only one 'toilet' for everybody, and the prisoners were not permitted to receive any news from the outside world, either from loved ones or by way of newspapers; they were utterly isolated. However, almost all of the prisoners at Taganskaya were either important political or social activists, or academics, and being with each other gave them inner strength – they often managed to give lectures in their own specialities in between tortuous interrogations. According to Doctor Samet, one of my father's cellmates, my father taught an entire course on 'hygiene in the workplace' while imprisoned at Taganskaya. Despite a terrible sense of disquiet caused by the absence of news from his loved ones, he managed to maintain his composure and remained courageously upbeat. However, deep down he feared that his wife had also been arrested, and he worried desperately for me, his pregnant daughter.

My mother and I spent most of this time waiting in long

queues outside Taganskaya Prison in the hope of finding out anything at all about my father and trying to give him a food parcel and some money. However, no news about the prisoners was forthcoming.

On 25 May 1938, Father was charged with espionage and sentenced by an NKVD troika to eight years in a corrective labour camp.

Towards the end of May, Investigator Chernov called my mother to tell her that 'Tieits S.' was being sent to a corrective labour camp in the Far East. For days and nights on end my mother and I waited at Moscow's Kazan railway station alongside crowds of others just like us, in the hope of catching a glimpse of Father. Scores of cargo wagons lined the platforms, preparing to transport the prisoners away. We were chased away from the trains repeatedly, but nonetheless continued to run back towards them in the hope of seeing my father. We never did see him though.

The first news came on 21 July. A small, empty packet of cigarettes appeared in our postbox, marked with our address. Inside was an unravelled cigarette butt made from papyrus, on which was written:

> Moscow 21/VII. My darlings! Today I am leaving
> Moscow for Kolyma. Happy Birthday Ninochka! Take
> care of yourselves, don't worry about me. Give my best
> to everybody. Love, Samuil.

He had thrown this packet out of his train carriage and sympathetic, understanding people (there were countless other people suffering the very same tragedy) somehow ensured that the letter reached us.

As time went on, similar notes began to arrive from various points along the train's long route east: from Noginsk, Saratov, Omsk . . . This nightmarish journey in freight wagons packed

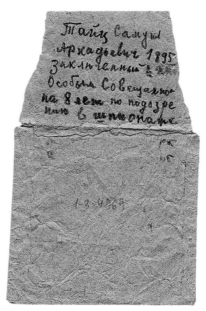

Samuil Tieits, Vladivostok,
1938.

An envelope from a letter sent to his
family from a labour camp; inside the flap
he was obliged to write his name, the
charges against him and his sentence.

with the sick, dying, dead, starving and thirsty, lying on floors
and shelves, lasted for months on end, as the train wended
its way towards Vladivostok. They stood for hours under the
burning sun as the train crossed the steppe, and Father fell
ill with a severe bout of scurvy. In an amateur photograph
that he later sent from Vladivostok, he was unrecognisable.
He looked old, and his face and hands were swollen and filled
with fluid.

On arrival in Vladivostok he was sent to the camp hospital,
and was later transferred to the transit point of the NKVD
SVITlag,* where he was allocated to the fifth barracks of the
third work brigade.

---

* Translator's note: SVITlag is an acronym for North-Eastern Corrective Labour
Camps. As such, this particular transit point (*tranzitka*) was a distribution point
for the labour camps in Kolyma, where thousands of prisoners awaited onward
transportation.

We were absolutely certain that my mother would be arrested too. For several years she kept a suitcase at the ready, packed with all the essential items for prison, and every night she waited for them to come for her. I managed to convince her that nobody was ever arrested on a Sunday, as the NKVD took that day off. This 'white lie' allowed her to sleep soundly for one night per week.

My father sent us many letters from the transit points on his journey and despite the horrors of his situation, each and every one was staggeringly cheerful, and centred around his concern for us. The letters, written on brown parcel paper, were folded into home-made envelopes, inside which he had been obliged to write, 'Tieits S. A. 1895. Serving 8 years in a corrective labour camp on charges of espionage.'

In an extract from a letter to my mother he writes:

> I implore you to write frequent, detailed letters to me, as I
> want to be kept well informed with unvarnished accounts
> of your day-to-day life. You must be having to work so
> hard, my dear! If only I could do something to help you.
> I would like to hope that my situation will soon change.
> In any case, we need to take the necessary steps to ensure
> that my statement of appeal is read, but since there is
> no case against me, there cannot even be anything to
> consider. (26.05.1939)

The 'case' really had been contrived hurriedly and clumsily. In a statement to the chairman of the Presidium of the Supreme Soviet, Nikolai Shvernik, my father wrote:

> During the interrogation I was told in no uncertain
> terms that I could not be released from custody and
> must personally come up with some sort of reason for
> my arrest. At the very least, I was told, I must implicate

myself in espionage. When I refused to invent a fictitious
story of this kind, Investigator Holdanov gave me a
book containing material intended to jog my memory.
The book was entitled 'On the activities of spying
organisations in the USSR' and had been written by the
then-director of the Moscow branch of the NKVD and
Deputy Commissar of Internal Affairs, Leonid Zakovsky.*
(Incidentally, it was on Zakovsky's orders that I was
arrested.) The investigator told me that I needed to
choose an example of espionage from the cases in this
book and incriminate myself. As a result of measures of
physical violence used against me, I was forced to sign a
false self-confession in the hope that its absurdity would
be plain for everyone to see. I hoped that once I was out
of the clutches of the investigator, who had employed
un-Soviet methods while leading the investigation, the
blatantly groundless nature of my self-confession would be
obvious, and my innocence easy to prove.

From Vladivostok, my father was sent to Magadan, Kolyma.
There were several gold mines in the area; at Ust-Utinaya,
Nizhny Seymchan and Duskanya, and almost immediately he
was put to work as a doctor, treating both prisoners and free
workers in the camp. Meanwhile, I was studying at the Medical
Institute, and in his letters my father worried about the standard
of my work, endeavouring to provide his expert guidance as I

---

* Leonid Zakovsky was one of the chief perpetrators of the Great Terror
between 1920 and 1930 (in Siberia, Belarus, Leningrad and Moscow). From
20 January 1938 to 28 March 1938, he was director of the NKVD Directorate
for the Moscow region and at the same time (29 January 1938 to 1 April 1938)
he was Deputy Commissar of Internal Affairs. He was shot on 29 August 1938.
Presumably here Tieits is referring to one of Zakovsky's pamphlets published
by Partizdat in 1937, e.g. 'We will eliminate spies, saboteurs and enemies' and
'About some of the methods and measures employed by foreign intelligence
agencies and their Trotskyist-Bukharinsky agencies'.

weighed up my professional options. I do not need to comment on these letters; they speak for themselves.

> My darling Ninushechka! [. . .] How are your studies going? How did you get on in your exams? I would like to know everything. [. . .] Are you enjoying studying at the nursing faculty? It is difficult to advise you from here, but if possible it would be better for you to transfer to the department of medicine. (24.04.1939)

> My darling Ninochka,
> You are now beginning your third year, an extremely significant phase in any doctor's training. I don't know what speciality you will choose – I hope that we will be able to talk a little more about this in person. However, there is one thing that you must bear in mind. Life can cast you far away (sometimes this may correspond with your dearest wishes in life and sometimes, as in my case, it may not and you may be forced to travel) and you must be ready to carry out the most diverse medical work, not simply limited to your own narrow specialism. In short, you must take an active interest in all subjects and get a good all-round education. (08.11.1939)

> Ninochka, my golden girl. I just cannot believe that you are now in your 3rd year and are already so seriously engaged in the work of a doctor. This very year you will start going to clinics and studying a whole ream of clinical subjects. I do not doubt that you will study enthusiastically and rather than confining your reading to your textbooks alone, you will also read literature on the founders of medicine. [. . .] I would really like you to become a doctor with a broad educational foundation, and not just a medic by trade. The knowledge and

perspective acquired during your student years broadens your horizons and plays a very important part in determining the skills and interests of a doctor later in life. You must also acquire technical skills, regardless of the specialism for which you are preparing. A narrow specialism is fine in the city, but you may choose to live somewhere out in the Taiga and there you may need to give medical assistance in the most varied of circumstances . . . (04.10.1939)

My dearest Ninochka! [. . .] Now that you are already in your fourth year and the odds of you passing your exams are in your favour, it is time to ask yourself what you would like to specialise in. I hope you won't mind me giving my advice on this matter. Although you are studying at the nursing faculty, and it seems that this will define your future speciality, you absolutely must acquire as much knowledge as possible on medical treatment practices while you are still at the institute. A narrow speciality can only support you in a city – as soon as you are in the countryside or villages you need to be able to do everything, or at the very least have many different specialities. What if you are sent on a placement when you finish university or you choose to live somewhere other than Moscow? If that happens, you will need to know how to treat patients too, especially since ordinary people are of the opinion that if a person is to call himself a doctor, he or she must always be capable of offering medical assistance. [. . .] And it is absolutely essential to choose your speciality while you are still in your final year and to work hard at it (without forgoing any of the others), so that by the time you finish at the institute, your head of department recognises you as an exemplary student and is willing to provide the necessary support. (09.07.1940)

Reading these letters, one cannot fail to be struck by how persistently my father offered his advice, insisting that I acquire a broad base of knowledge through an all-encompassing approach to my training, rather than confining myself to one speciality alone. His advice was not without design. Though he always wrote of this indirectly, he made absolutely sure that I understood that a person must be ready for any twist of fate; one that could send them far from Moscow, 'somewhere out in the Taiga' not only on business, but perhaps 'for some other reason'. In such circumstances, an all-round medical education could prove a matter of life and death. When I settled for a job as a regional public health doctor for the sake of the salary while I finished my studies at the institute, he was far from pleased.

> Nina's decision to work in the public health domain
> does not fill me with joy. During her first years of work,
> she absolutely must first and foremost get to grips with
> medical matters and obtain hands-on practice in this
> area. Administrative work can come later, for once she
> has the medical experience, this too will be much more
> useful and important. If there were any way to find some
> kind of permanent work in a hospital of some sort, this
> would be far more useful and she would be of much
> greater help to society. Or perhaps it might be possible
> to find her work in a science laboratory (at the institute)?
> (12.06.1943)

Right up until the end, my father remained firm in his belief that justice would be restored. As far as he was able, he tried to pass this hope on to my mother and me.

> I continue to believe that Fate's course will very soon be
> altered. [. . .] We need to be strong, and to hope that in
> the near future we will go back to living as we did before.

Where are the photographs that you promised me? I really wanted to see you and Ninochka, albeit just in prints for now. (31.08.1939)

I firmly believe that I will be coming home to you very soon. The only danger is that with the routes only navigable from 15 December to 15 May, there may not be enough time for the authorities to work through all the formalities and terms of my appeal. I do not doubt that the procurator's appeal will lead the NKVD to make a decision in my favour. (09.10.1939)

I live in the hope that we will soon see each other again and return to our former lives. How is my golden daughter? She will have more time in the summer – perhaps she can write to me then. (22.06.1940)

I am absolutely certain that this will all end soon, and with the outcome we desire. (04.11.1940)

Fate was not to grant him his wishes. Papa died suddenly from a brain haemorrhage in October 1944 at the age of forty-nine. Three months earlier, I received this letter from him:

Ninochka, my darling. From your letters I understand that you are currently preparing and training to become a radiologist. This is not a bad speciality, but it demands a greater depth of knowledge than many others because other doctors approach a radiologist when they have their doubts about a diagnosis. Your conclusion will very often be definitive, and from it a further course of treatment will be determined. As a result, it is vital to be a fully qualified radiologist and not to limit your knowledge to technology alone. (24.07.1944)

I fulfilled my father's last wishes. After graduating from the Medical Institute, I wrote my Candidate of Science thesis and worked until my retirement in 1975 as manager of the Radiology Department in the medicinal nutrition clinic at the Academy of Medical Science's Institute of Nutrition.

My father was posthumously rehabilitated in 1955. After the rehabilitation, his brother, Max and I installed memorial plaques bearing my father and Uncle David's names at the bottom of the Donsk Crematorium graveyard, the final resting place of my grandmother and grandfather.

I dedicated my memoirs, *Life's Line in Letters and Documents: 1895–1944: A Daughter's Memoirs* (Moscow, 2006), to my father. The book contains my memories, documents from his 'case file', and letters sent from the Kolyma Gulag. In my opinion, these documents and letters are of great historical importance. It is vital to preserve them for today's generations and for the generations to come. They beseech people to ensure that nothing of this sort ever occurs again.

Armin Stromberg

'Do you know what saved me? Letters.
The connection with home.'

Armin Heinrichovich Stromberg (1910–2004) wrote
letters to his wife and daughter
from 1942 to 1943 while
imprisoned in the Nizhny
Tagilsky NKVD camp, where
he had been sent solely on
account of his having been
born to a German father.

Armin Stromberg, Tomsk, 1992.

Armin's father, an associate professor at the Military Medical
Academy in St Petersburg, had run a military field hospital
during the early stages of the First World War until his death in
1914. After the death of her husband, his mother moved home
to Yekaterinburg to raise her two young children.

On finishing school, Stromberg enrolled at the Chemistry
Faculty of the Ural Polytechnic Institute in 1927, where he
completed an accelerated chemistry degree, graduating in 1930.
He then began his working life in the Institute of Chemistry
and Metallurgy at the Ural branch of the USSR Academy of
Sciences.

In an extract from his memoirs, Armin Stromberg writes:

During my third year at the institute (in 1929), and in line with the beginning of the first 'five year plan' (1930), the motto 'human resources decide everything' was coined, and the order was given to 'accelerate the graduation' of every student in higher education. As a result, instead of studying for five years, I spent only three and half at the institute. In May 1930, at just nineteen years old, I graduated as a certified 'engineer-chemist' (I had specialised in electrochemistry). Of course, I never wrote a thesis, and my technical knowledge was a little hit and miss. Fortunately though, this absence of technical knowledge did not hamper me in life as I was immediately assigned to the Scientific Research Institute and never once worked in a factory. But I did find my depth of understanding in the general disciplines (physical chemistry in particular) to be insufficient. As a result, as soon as I graduated from the institute, I set about educating myself further . . .

Armin Stromberg's efforts were borne out by his achievements, and by 1939 he had obtained a Candidate of Science degree. His life seemed to be falling into place, but in an interview with the *Tomsk Vestnik* in 1991, Stromberg recalled that 'a sense of danger arose in the second half of the 30s'. He described an episode from his own experiences of this time:

In 1937 a group of students arrived from Leningrad* University to undertake an internship at the Institute. I rather liked one of the girls, Lydia Poponina, and I plucked up the courage to tell her how I felt. The other students were horrified when they found out that Lydia intended to marry a German. Leningrad was experiencing a wave of arrests around that time and they tried to talk her out

* Today St Petersburg.

Armin Stromberg with his wife, Lydia, and daughter, Elza, Sverdlovsk, 22 June 1941.

of it. She, however, was not frightened. We signed the marriage register in the summer of 1937, without holding a ceremony . . . (30.05.1991)

A daughter was born in 1938, and the music-loving young parents named her Elza, after the heroine in Wagner's opera. In her memoirs Elza Zakharova writes:

> Sunday 22 June 1941 was a carefree day spent relaxing together as a family. We had our photograph taken, blissfully unaware of what lay ahead. The frightening early days of war were upon us though, and all German families living in the European portion of the USSR were either being sent east, or to the North Ural regions. We were among those who received orders to leave. Fortunately, however, my father's mother, Magda, a beautiful and vivacious woman and former student of the Bestuzhev Courses, had been one of the very first chemistry teachers in the Urals and happened to have taught a number of Party members. One of her former pupils was the director of the Ural Polytechnic

Institute, a man called Kachko, who came to the aid of our family. But in March 1942 my father was called up to join the Trudarmii (Labour Army) . . .*

Armin Stromberg writes in his memoirs:

A messenger arrived with a signed note informing me that I had been 'mobilised into the ranks of the Workers' and Peasants' Red Army' (as a qualified scientist at the Institute, I should have been exempt). All those gathered at the *voenkomat*† were Germans. We were informed that we had been mobilised into the Labour Army and were ordered to return the following day with our belongings. We were then packed into *platzkart*‡ train carriages and transported to the NKVD Gulag (special German detachment Number 1874), behind the barbed wire at the brick factory in the city of Nizhny Tagil.

Conditions at this special detachment camp were very harsh. According to data from a number of sources, in three years 3,000 of the 6,000-strong population of this German Labour Army died from cold, hunger and the unendurable work conditions . . .

In his interview with the *Tomsk Vestnik* Stromberg said:

Hunger – that was most frightening of all. From morning until night, we thought of one thing only – how to get hold of food. [. . .] I'm embarrassed to admit that to this day, I still have an inherent fear of finding myself without it. At home,

---

* The Labour Army – see Index of Places of Imprisonment.
† Voenkomat(s): A network of local military administrative centres responsible for military recruitment and mobilisation.
‡ Open-plan train carriages with tiered bunks (the equivalent to today's 'third class' train carriage in Russia).

if I see that we are running low on bread, I take my grocery
bag and go to the bakery [. . .]. Do you know what saved
me? Letters. The connection with home. (30.05.1991)

During his time in the camp, Stromberg sent his wife and
daughter 74 letters, which amounted to a minimum of one or
two letters per week.

> Lidusenka! I have been at N. Tagil for eight days now,
> and this is the eighth time that I have sat down to write
> to you. They must be laughing at me, for writing home
> so often, but I just feel compelled to do so. When I am
> writing, I feel as though I am chatting to you, and I am
> transported back to our life all together . . . (28.03.1942)

Stromberg often directed parts of the letters directly to his
little daughter, asking her questions, writing separate pages
to her or including a note at the end of his letters. He also
drew pictures for her, and these were later glued into an album
and given to her on her birthday. 'Lidusenka,' he wrote to his
wife, 'write and tell me more about Elzochka. I have acquired
an album (exercise book) for her in which I am copying out
extracts from letters about her.'
In her memoirs Elza Zakharova writes:

> Sometime in the 80s, my father showed me a thick packet
> of faded letters. It transpired that he had saved each of the 74
> letters that he had written to my mother during his years in
> the Labour Army between 1942 and 1943. It was not until
> Perestroika, and his rehabilitation in 1993, that a printed
> explanation emerged, detailing what exactly this Labour
> Army was. We learned that 'work brigade 1874' had been
> interned in the city of Nizhny Tagil, behind the barbed
> wire at one of the many 'Gulag Archipelago' labour camps.

A page from the album created by Stromberg for his daughter. It was entitled: 'Correspondence from a mobilised father (N. Tagil) to his daughter Elzochka (Sverdlovsk), March 1942–September 1943'.

Prior to this, I had no idea that my father's collection of letters even existed – they were just wrapped in paper and tied up with string alongside some scientific papers and a few other documents at home.

As a child, nobody ever talked to me about my father's absence – it was simply an accepted fact that he had served in the army, and there was nothing to show for those years. Indeed, our relatives tried to forget all about them, pushing them to the back of their minds as if they had been a nightmarish dream. It seems that my father completely forgot about the letters too; he never reread them and I remember that he was utterly shocked when he looked through them again fifty years later.

Stromberg's letters were written in ink on the rough paper used for baking bricks at the camp or on paper torn from sacks of cement. They were posted in envelopes or folded into triangles with stamps attached and, of course, each letter had to pass through camp military censorship, as evidenced by the official stamps on the envelopes and the black lines striking out certain sentences.

> Papa was a very loving father. When I was born he ordered a thick album with a red cardboard cover with my name on it (as was the tradition in German families) in which he recorded all the changes that he observed in my development. He stuck in photos (he loved photography) and a variety of drawings. He wanted my mother to keep all the letters in which he described his work and living conditions, and in an attempt to keep up to date with family goings-on, he often asked about the mundane aspects of daily life that had fallen to my mother and grandmother to handle. He wrote everything intended for me on separate pieces of paper, and glued them into my album alongside drawings, continuing to do so until I reached school age. I was always interested to see what father had written or drawn for me. A well-known artist imprisoned in the same camp allowed him to borrow his coloured pencils, so many of the drawings he sent me were watercolours, sometimes even painted on filter paper!

According to Stromberg, he only survived the camp because he managed to transfer from 'general labour' to an administrative position as a dispatcher in the firing workshop at the brick factory, and later as a supervisor in the quality control unit. He spent a year and a half at the camp before being returned, in September 1943, to the very same institute from which he had been 'mobilised'. With him he carried a note bearing a very unusual message for that time: 'At your disposal is Stromberg, Armin Heinrichovich, demobilised from detachment number 1874 so as to be put to use in his field of specialism'.

The other unfortunate German Labour Army prisoners who remained in the camp until the end of the war found themselves stranded in Nizhny Tagil for a further ten years following their demobilisation; they were labelled as 'special settlers without the right to leave the city'.

Below are a few extracts from Stromberg's letters home:

> My darling daughter,
> How are things with you? Have you started kindergarten?
> Your Papa is in the army at the moment, but he isn't
> shooting the Fascists with rifles and bullets. Instead he
> is making bricks for the factories that will make tanks,
> aeroplanes, cannons and bombs. Listen to your mother,
> sweetheart. It is very difficult for her at the moment
> without Papa. Help her. Dress yourself, and don't be
> difficult at mealtimes. Go to kindergarten. Don't fight
> with Vitya. If he upsets you, then tell him that you will
> write to your Papa in the army and tell him about it.
> Then write me a letter. Do some drawing with coloured
> pencils: a man, a tank, an aeroplane. [. . .] Goodbye
> darling. Your Papa loves you very much and wants to see
> you. But he isn't allowed to leave the army because he
> has been mobilised. When the war is over and the Fascists
> have been defeated, Papa will come home and kiss his
> little daughter again and again. Your Papa (March 1942)

> It must be so hard for you, Lidusya, all on your own. I
> would gladly share the effort of raising our daughter but I
> can do nothing to help. She is now at an interesting age.
> I so regret that I was preoccupied with work during the
> months before I left and didn't pay her much attention.
> Now I imagine all the time that my daughter is sitting on

A letter to his daughter,
27.03.1942.

my knee and I picture her writing the words and drawing
the tanks that I see in the letters you send me. My sweet,
beloved daughter. Will I see her again soon? (April 1942)

I remember, I remember so well that it is our daughter's
birthday on 5 May. I am sending her a birthday card.
I feel ashamed that I have so upset my little girl by not
writing often enough. It is just astonishing that such little
people can worry in the way that grown-ups do. It is
such a shame that I cannot attend my little girl's birthday
party and join in the celebrations. She is now at the most
interesting age. (May 1942)

Lidusenka, yesterday I received your letter, parcel and
Elza's many drawings . . . thank you so very much. I am
just sorry that you sent me the meagre crumbs that you

and our daughter receive from your ration cards. Don't do that again [. . .] Write and tell me more about our daughter. I studied the picture that she drew at length, and deduced that she had drawn a house (with the window separate), and a bed with a quilt and pillow. I couldn't make out what the 4 pictures above were meant to show. Ask Elza to draw pictures especially for me and explain them to you . . . (November 1942)

Will I see my little daughter again soon? Write and tell me about her – about the phrases she is using, her escapades, and all the mischief. It's interesting to hear how she perceives reality and views these challenging times of war – what is her attitude to war and to the fascist invaders? Take note Lidusya, and write it all down for me in a letter. For I have been deprived of the chance to see my daughter develop, and even if I do get to see her, in one year let's say, she will doubtless be completely different from how she is now, aged four and a half . . . (November 1942)

Stromberg sometimes drew comic sketches on his letters. On the reverse of one such note depicting little Elza playing with a tank while sitting on her father's knee, is written:

My sweet daughter,
Here I have drawn a picture showing Papa returning home after the war, bringing you a toy tank as a present. Elzochka is so delighted at her Papa's return. She gathers the tank into her arms and climbs onto his knee. Her Papa strokes his daughter's hair and tells her how much he

has missed her and how happy he is that he can now be with her again. (November 1942)

He requested that Elza send him her own drawings in return, and asked what games she enjoyed playing, what she was reading and other questions about her life.

My sweet little daughter – Elzochka.
I received your drawings: a mushroom, a tree, a little house, Mama and Papa pushing Elzochka in her pram. Draw some more pictures for me and ask Mama to send them to me [. . .]. Which books are you reading? What new toys do you have? I'm very interested to hear all this. I am sending you a big kiss, my beloved daughter. Your Papa (April 1943)

My sweet daughter,
Thank you for your drawing. You drew the two-storey

Left: Elza Stromberg during her first year at primary school (aged 7), Sverdlovsk. 02.09.1945. *Right:* A drawing from a letter, June 1943.

Picture enclosed with a letter, June 1943.

house behind the fence so well. It makes your Papa very happy to hear that you are helping your mother by washing the floor, clearing the table and tidying up your toys. What new toys do you have? Do you have any dolls? Any dresses for them? A bed, table, chair? What games do you play with your dolls? Who do you play with? Where will you go to the dacha this summer? Write and tell me. I'm sending you a kiss. Papa. (June 1943)

After his liberation from the Nizhny Tagil camp, Armin Stromberg lived a long and very learned life until his death at the age of ninety-four. In 1951 he completed a Doctor of Sciences* degree, and five years later he moved to Tomsk, where he ran the Physical and Colloid Chemistry Department at Tomsk Polytechnic Institute for thirty years. In total, he prepared eighty-seven students of Chemical Science for Candidate of Science degrees and four students for Doctor of Science degrees.

Stromberg also founded and ran a research laboratory specifically dedicated to finding trace impurities in different

---

* The Doctor of Sciences is a higher doctoral degree that can be earned following the completion of a Candidate of Sciences degree.

materials and wrote a textbook on physical chemistry for higher education, which was published in seven editions. He became a member of the Scientific Committee of the Russian Academy of Sciences on Analytical Chemistry and, in addition to being decorated with medals and awards, he went on to be awarded the title of Honoured Chemist of the Russian Federation.

Unsurprisingly, however, his time in the NKVD camp left its mark upon him. For the rest of his life, Armin Stromberg suffered from 'second-class citizen syndrome', although in this too he managed to find a positive angle. In his memoirs he writes:

> *The position of a 'second-class citizen' came with its own social and national benefits too:*
>
> 1. I was not put forward for administrative duties, which left me with more time to further my own professional knowledge.
> 2. I always understood that in order to be on the same level in the scientific world as those who were 'socially accepted',[*] I needed to be a head higher in terms of professional knowledge (for example, to have a Doctor of Science qualification when among those with a Candidate of Science degree). This forced me to constantly further my knowledge in my chosen scientific field and to achieve more than I would have done had the scientific community 'laid out a carpet under my feet'.

Stromberg's motto for life was a phrase coined by the Russian-Soviet agronomist Nikolai Vavilov: 'Life is short. So hurry.' According to his students, Stromberg never squandered time – he kept it closely 'under supervision'. He appreciated

---

[*] i.e. having proletarian roots.

it, managed it and analysed it. No time was left 'unused' – it was filled with carefully planned and controlled activities. Unforeseen events and circumstances would knock him completely out of his rhythm, for he lived according to a strict regime. If he planned a meeting for 09.00 he would be completely thrown if the student arrived at 09.15. He wrote out study plans for his students in an exercise book and marked assignments diligently. For many years, he noted down exactly how he had spent his time in a thick daily planner. Four diaries have survived: from 1975–6, 1976–8, 1980–81 and 1981–2. On every page he described his day, hour by hour, and at the end of each day he would note the day's results (in hours): hours spent on science, on organisational-scientific matters, on reading. He also reported 'events'. In his final years, Stromberg noted things down irregularly, but he continued to live by his customary routine, never breaking from it. In his memoirs he wrote:

> I have lived a long life. I am now reaching the end of my long scientific road, surrounded by my students and, in general, I have no complaints about the life I have lived.

Stromberg's wife, Lydia (1912–72), worked in the Physics Department of the Ural Polytechnic Institute from 1937–56. When the family moved to Tomsk, she taught at the Physics Department of Tomsk Polytechnic Institute. His daughter, Elza Zakharova, followed in her father's footsteps, completing a Candidate of Science degree in chemical science and becoming a senior lecturer at Tomsk State University. She spent the final twenty years of her life working as a senior research fellow at Tomsk Polytechnic University. His granddaughter, Olga Stromberg, took her grandfather's name and works as a haematologist in Stockholm.

Nikolai Lyubchenko

'Just don't you, or our little son, forget me'

Nikolai Petrovich Lyubchenko, or Mikola, as his family called him, was arrested on 5 December 1934 and charged with affiliation to a counter-revolutionary organisation of Ukrainian nationalists. He was sentenced by the Military Collegium of the USSR Supreme Court to ten years' 'deprivation of liberty' and initially sent to the Karlag, before being transferred to the labour camp at Solovki in 1936.

Nikolai Petrovich Lyubchenko, late 1920s.

The letters that Nikolai Lyubchenko sent to his wife, Vera, and son Oleg (affectionately known as 'Lesik' or 'Olesik') from these places of incarceration were stored away and preserved until 2007, when Oleg published them in a book entitled *'Just don't you, or our little son, forget me.'** Oleg's book also contains his father's 'Grey Notebook', in which Lyubchenko noted down the poems that he composed while imprisoned in the Gulag between December 1935 and January 1936.

---

* Lyubchenko, M. P., *Just Don't You or Our Little Son Forget Me* (M. Sputnik, 2007).

Vera Lyubchenko with son Oleg, 1933.

Nikolai Lyubchenko with Oleg, Kharkov, 1934.

Unfortunately, relatively little is known of Lyubchenko's life prior to his arrest. He was born in 1896 and studied at Kiev University, although he never actually graduated, choosing instead to abandon his books in favour of joining the Revolution. A committed Bolshevik, he became an active member of the underground movement, thus playing his part in his country's metamorphosis during the years of Civil War. After the Revolution, Lyubchenko worked in the editorial team of the *Communist* newspaper, where he was head of the Department of Information before being appointed to run the newspaper's feuilleton.* He was also a member of the newspaper's editorial board and, in addition to devising satirical leaflets, he wrote columns and composed humoresques. Several of his essays and short stories were published under his pseudonym, Kost Kotko.

Little else is known, other than at some point, Lyubchenko

---

* A satirical supplement chiefly devoted to reviews, poetry and serialised fiction.

worked in the diplomatic service as First Secretary and adviser to the Soviet envoy in Warsaw and Prague. According to his wife, he also headed the All-Ukrainian Society of Cultural Ties with Foreign Countries.

When Vera Lyubchenko went to visit her husband in the Karlag, he told her that during the interrogation, the NKVD investigator had coerced him into denouncing the chairman of the Ukrainian Council of People's Commissars, his namesake, Panas Lyubchenko. Since Panas was head of government of the Ukrainian Soviet Socialist Republic at the time, the investigator conducting the interrogation did not ask this of Lyubchenko directly. Instead, he wrote 'Panas' on his pad of blotting paper and inadvertently, so to speak, coerced Nikolai into incriminating him.

The conditions inside the NKVD prison in Kiev were comparatively good. Judging by Lyubchenko's short letters, he even began to indulge in a little literary creativity while incarcerated there; he began writing a book about Czechoslovakia and composed poems based on fairy tales for his son. It is as likely as not that the 'leniency' extended towards Lyubchenko arose from a sense of sympathy on the part of the investigator, who was well aware that his prisoner was entirely innocent. Whatever his motives, Vera remembers that even before the court had reached a verdict on her husband's case following his arrest, this same investigator had urged her to leave Kiev. In doing so he undoubtedly saved Vera from imminent arrest, and her young son from growing up in a state orphanage.

Lyubchenko's son recalls a little from this period in his memoirs:

> In early May 1935, a little over a month after the court handed down their sentence, my father was put on a train east to the Karagandinsky Labour Camp (Karlag). His sisters in Kiev found out that he was to be transported via Moscow,

where my mother and I were then living temporarily, and they managed to get word to us to this effect. We were told what time and day (5 May) the train would be arriving and they said that it was likely we would be able to obtain permission to meet.

I do not remember my father being taken – I hadn't yet turned three years old. In the five months that followed his arrest, however, I grew a little older and somehow began to make sense of some things in my head. I remember the meeting at Moscow's Kievsky Railway Station particularly clearly. I can still see his figure on the railway platform now; not very tall, slight, coatless but wearing a plain suit, albeit with a jumper on over the top of his suit jacket. I, of course, did not understand that he was being transported away, and paid no attention to the escort guards. I looked at him alone. Without pausing to wait for us, he walked quickly along the platform beside the train carriages and we followed him a little way behind. I then remember a dark and crowded room inside the station. My father was sitting behind a large table . . . he spoke to us, asked me about something, and I said something in reply. I remember this moment very clearly. The meeting did not last long; in all likelihood we were there only ten minutes before we parted. My mother later visited him at the Karlag, but I never saw my father again.

This is what he wrote about our meeting in the little grey notebook addressed to me: 'You ran after me, looking miserable and dejected, crying: "Papa, Papa!" You didn't understand why your Papa was leaving you. And then in the guards' room you asked, "Do you work here?"'

According to his son, Nikolai Lyubchenko kept up continuous correspondence with his family from within the camp. However, only a very few letters remain out of the tens that he sent. In almost every letter, he addressed several lines to his little son, Lesik.

> Lesinka, I am going to send you and your mother a
> new fairy tale. We have lots of camels here – all with
> two humps. There is one who thinks he is a steam train,
> and decided to run off down the railway line. It was
> very funny! I want to write a fairy tale about him . . .
> (26.12.1935)

> . . . I have not yet managed to finish writing the fairy tale
> for you, so am sending you just the very beginning:

>> The steppe is covered with prickly Caragana
>> The steppe is covered, like storm clouds, with caravans.
>> Camel follows along behind camel,
>> Atop the camels ride all sorts of folk
>> Atop the camels perch all sorts of loads.

> I have written a few poems for you in my notebook . . .
> (11.01.1936)

> My sweet, beloved son, my darling Olesik! You are
> already five years old. How quickly a year has passed.
> A boy gets bigger and bigger and before long he is fully
> grown and clever. Mama tells me that you are a very
> good boy, but that you sometimes upset her by not
> listening. You mustn't do that, my Olesik. You must love
> your Mama dearly. [. . .]
> And remember too, that all children in Moscow, and
> in Lugansk and in Kharkov and in Yasnaya Polyana –
> everywhere, everywhere – must love Stalin, who wishes
> the very best to all Soviet children, and all children
> everywhere . . . (12.01.1937)

It may well be that the letters he sent home were written with an eye cast to the camp censorship. However, there is no reason to believe that their contents are insincere or in any way artificial. The 'little grey notebook' as his son refers to it, confirms all that he wrote. The notebook contains handwritten text penned by Lyubchenko during his time in the NKVD Kiev Prison and at the Karlag, from 8 December 1934 until 10 January 1936. This notebook did not pass through camp censorship – Lyubchenko handed it to his wife when she came to visit him at the camp.

The notebook is filled with poems and fairy-tale rhymes written by Lyubchenko for his son, as he sought to play his own small part in Oleg's upbringing. They included 'Lullaby', 'Mutiny of the Toys', 'Elephant in the Bus', 'Lesik Goes to Moscow', a humorous rhyme entitled 'Lady Prisya' and one unfinished poem, 'Ai-Soluk'. Oleg recalls that the poems his father sent were read to him so often that many lines are still firmly imprinted in his memory.

It was inevitable, however, that the unfounded arrest and separation from his family would impact upon the notebook's contents. The first poem, 'Lullaby', was written on 8 December 1934, just three days after his arrest. Nikolai Lyubchenko accompanied the poem with a short note to his son:

> A few days before 5 December I was cutting your hair and one gorgeous curl found its way into my pocket (of sweater). I was wearing this sweater when I left. On 8 December I found this curl by chance! What a comfort and support it has been to me! How I pounced on a pencil, when I was finally given one, to write down the words that came to me the moment that I found that lock of hair.

> Hush, little one,
> Close your eyes and sleep –

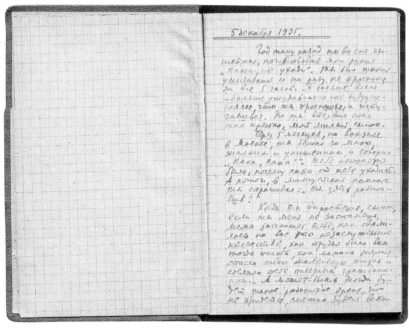

An entry in Nikolai Lyubchenko's 'Grey Notebook', 05.12.1935.

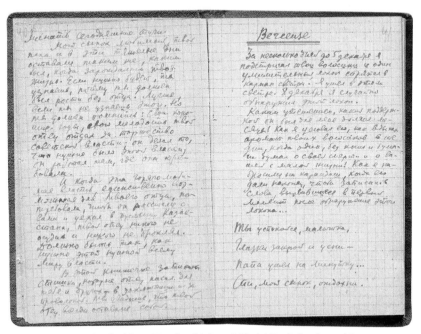

A message in the 'Grey Notebook' from Nikolai Lyubchenko to his son.

> Papa has gone for a minute . . .
> Sleep my son, rest . . .

Lyubchenko's letters to his wife always contained lines addressed to his son. These he wrote in capital letters.

> My darling Verochka! I don't quite know what to say to you. I fear that the letters I sent you in August (I didn't write in July) did not reach you. The last letter that I received from you was dated 24 August, when you were getting ready to leave the dacha. I haven't the slightest idea how you both are, whether you are healthy or if our son is learning to read and write.
>
> As for me, everything is just the same as before. I am not working at the moment, but they are feeding me nonetheless, so I have no need of anything. I can make do without parcels, as I mentioned earlier. I am in good health. The warm summer has helped – my feet don't hurt even in the rain. You absolutely must write to me twice a month – I have been despondent without news from you.
>
> I have made the most of any free time to gather together all the letters that you have written about our son over the past year and a half. It has been very interesting to follow his development. He must be able to read a few short stories by now. MY SWEET SON OLESIK! WRITE ME A LETTER. LOVE YOUR MOTHER AND TAKE CARE OF HER, BUT DON'T FORGET YOUR PAPA. YOUR PAPA LOVES YOU VERY MUCH AND THINKS ABOUT YOU EVERY MINUTE.
>
> You will need to write to the address given on the envelope. I repeat it here:
>
> Kem, Kirovsky Railway, P.O Box 20/6.
>
> I am sending you a big kiss, Your M. (19.09.1937)

My darlings! I had already begun to worry that your
next letter would not reach me in time for the last May
post . . . but yesterday I received two: a letter from 04.04
and a postcard dated 22.04. I received the April parcel in
the very first batch, and the money too – 25r.

It is raining today so we do not have to work. By 10
o' clock this morning I had returned to our dormitory.
Almost everybody else is on duty, but I am writing a
letter. The weather is beginning to clear up – I think
that we will work tomorrow (agriculture, as you know,
depends on the weather).

Your letter contained 3 stamps, an envelope and 2
of Olesik's drawings. You need to state what you have
enclosed in the letter itself – that will avoid any mix-ups.

I really enjoyed reading what you wrote about our
son. Providing your words are not the exaggeration and
bias of a devoted mother, then by the sound of it our
Olesik will grow into a very interesting boy. Will such a
disposition make life easier for him though? Isn't it better
when people are self-confident and not just incapable of
admitting their own failings, but better still, completely
unaware of them? I have always envied those people who
never awake in the night thinking regretfully, 'Today I
didn't do this or that quite right.' I envy those who, upon
reading something typed by their own hand, never chew
their fingernails and think, 'How poor it still sounds, how
far from perfection. How much work it still requires!'
Moreover, at least among my own peers and friends, those
who I 'envied' proved to be the most successful. (I write
'envy' in inverted commas because of course I was not
jealous, they merely surprised me.) But I do not regret the
critical relationship that I have with my own endeavours.
One should only bemoan a lack of such a critical
relationship . . . and anyway, by the time Olesik grows

up, mankind, having been re-educated, will have reached such a state of perfection that life for those people who are honest with themselves will become easier. In any case, I am very pleased to hear about my son's disposition, namely his honesty and his inability to inflict pain. There is only one thing that worries me: isn't he too young to display such qualities?

It is such a shame that my letter to him did not arrive. The fairy tale had this very topic at its heart – it warned against overconfidence and conceit.

MY OLESIK, I SENT YOU A FAIRY TALE A LONG TIME AGO BUT THE POSTMAN WASN'T VERY GOOD AND HE LOST THE LETTER. [. . .]

Sending you both a big kiss, M. (22.05.1937)

The injustice of the suffering that had befallen him and 'contempt for traitors and scum' were themes that Nikolai Lyubchenko had intended to develop in his unfinished poem 'Ai-Soluk'. Nevertheless, he never doubted the righteousness of the Soviet state for a moment, and he wrote about this specifically in the messages to his son.

. . . When you grow up, my son, and if we do not meet, your mother will tell you how it was that this undeserved misfortune befell you both. [. . .] My darling son, even during these difficult days, your father remains the same man he was when you came into the world. If it must be so, then you will find out why you had to grow up without a father. It would be better if you were not to find out. But you must understand that your father surrendered your childhood and precious early years for the creation of the Soviet state. He did what this state required of him, and he worked where it commanded that he work. And when this most dearly beloved state, the only authority acceptable to your father, demanded that he be separated from you and that he go to the deserts of Kazakhstan, your father did not curse or condemn anybody. It had to be that way, as the state required it, this state of ours that the world so needs.

The poem 'Lullaby' that Lyubchenko wrote for his son concludes with the words: 'You must believe and remember – Papa will come home.' But Papa did not come home.

Nikolai Lyubchenko's son, Oleg (born 1932), chose to follow the same professional path as his father, graduating from the Journalism Faculty of the Lomonosov Moscow State University before pursuing a career in print media.

Anatoly Kozlovsky

'I loved you more than life'

Anatoly Kozlovsky (1897–1941) was shot at Oryol Prison on 11 September 1941.* Unfortunately, only one of a number of letters that he sent his wife and children has survived, hidden away in the family archives. It is not so much a letter as a 'message', sewn with thread onto a scrap of grey material that was most likely torn from the sheet of his prison bed. This truly unique and unusual note has become a family heirloom.

Anatoly Kozlovsky, 1920.

Anatoly Kozlovsky was born in Smolensk in 1897. His mother was a laundress, and though his father's profession is unknown, family lore states that he was some sort of seminarian at the Smolensk Theological College, where he apparently lodged with Anatoly's mother's family. Little more is known, other than the fact that Anatoly's mother fell pregnant, and his father was unable to marry her. As a result, the young mother gave birth to an illegitimate child, and it was

---

* 157 political prisoners held in Oryol Prison were shot on 11 September 1941, three weeks before the Germans arrived in the city. The executions were ordered by Stalin, as chairman of the State Defence Committee of the USSR.

decided that the little boy would be given the surname and patronymic of a local church elder and shoemaker.

Anatoly attended the parish primary school before moving to the Realschule to continue his education. When the First World War broke out, he volunteered to join the army but rather than being sent to the front, he was enrolled in the Officer Training College in Tbilisi, from where he graduated in 1918. As a result, it was not until the Civil War broke out that Kozlovsky was required to fight.

His daughter, Nina Kozlovskaya, remembers her mother's account of those years. Upon his graduation from the officer's college, her father had arrived in Smolensk in his brand new officer's uniform and almost immediately ran into a patrol of Red Army soldiers. 'Ah, you! You're a White. Remove your epaulettes,' they demanded. Kozlovsky immediately removed the offending epaulettes, threw them away and joined the Red Army. He served in its ranks for the duration of the Civil War, under the command of Tukhachevsky, before being wounded and awarded the Order of the Red Banner.*

In 1919, Kozlovsky married a girl from a very large Jewish family. Her name was Betty Slavina, and she was a typist working in the command headquarters. Nina was born in 1921, followed by a son four years later. They named him Engels.

By the time Engels was born, Kozlovsky was working for the OGPU as head of the border guard detachment responsible for controlling the Polish border. He was responsible for overseeing the fighting between Pavlovsky's platoon and that of Bulak Balachowicz in the disputed territory around the Polish border.

In an interview Nina Kozlovskaya said:

> I remember overhearing a conversation between my
> parents as a young girl. My mother said to my father,

---

* At this point in time, the Order of the Red Banner was the highest military award for bravery in Soviet Russia.

Anatoly Kozlovsky and his wife, Betty, 1920.

Betty Kozlovskaya with children Nina and Engels, Minsk, late 1920s.

'Tolya, do you remember that shtetl* we went to where those Jews had been hung from posts by their beards and young girls lay on the ground, with their breasts cut off?' My mother told me that a few years later she, my father and I had gone back to that same little town. There had been some kind of Jewish festival in full swing, and some respectable Jewish elders with full beards were sitting in the shade outside the synagogue. My mother told me that she and I had stood outside the synagogue, waiting for my father. All of a sudden he appeared, and all the Jews, the old men included, stood up and began bowing down to him, bending almost to the ground. He had saved them from the terrible pogroms during the Civil War.

In 1928, Kozlovsky was transferred to the OGPU Border Troops Directorate in Minsk, where he was soon promoted

---

* A small market-town with a large Jewish population formerly found in Central and Eastern Europe.

to head of the counter-intelligence service. He was arrested in 1937 while still working in this position.

Nina Kozlovskaya said:

> In 1935, Belarus was awarded the Order of Lenin, but in 1937 all of the Belarusian government officials – Chervyakov,* Goloded† and many others – were arrested. All of them! I was fourteen years old at the time and I asked my father, 'But Papa, how on earth can that happen? They had only just been decorated with medals for their good work, and now they are all "enemies of the people". How can that be?' My father looked at me for a long time, and then, avoiding eye contact, he said, 'It is hard for you to understand. I will say only this: when you grow up, you will understand everything.' By explaining nothing, my father was protecting me.

Kozlovsky was arrested in his office one evening while his wife and children were out at a concert. Knowing that having arrested him, the NKVD were likely to come for his wife, Kozlovsky managed to call home when she returned and tell her not to get undressed or go to sleep that night. According to his daughter, even before his arrest, Kozlovsky had warned their mother that she must 'be ready for anything'. 'I am guilty of nothing at all,' he told her, 'but you can see for yourself what is going on around us.' As he predicted, they came for his wife that very night.

---

* A. G. Chervyakov (1892–1937) was a member of the Central Committee of the Communist Party of Belarus (Bolsheviks). At the 16th session of the Communist Party, Chervyakov was strongly criticised for carrying out insufficient work on the elimination of 'enemies of the people'. He committed suicide shortly afterwards.

† N. M. Goloded (1894–1937) was chair of the Council of People's Commissars for the Belarusian Soviet Socialist Republic from 1927–37. He was arrested and during his interrogation at the NKVD building in Belarus he threw himself out of the window.

Following an investigation that lasted for two years, Kozlovsky was sentenced to death. Locked up in Minsk Prison, he waited day after day to be shot. Forbidden from corresponding with anybody on the outside, the resourceful father began to 'sew' a message for his family, using a fishbone that he presumably sourced from his prison rations, as a needle. This was difficult work, and Kozlovsky worried that he might not finish in time. Well aware that his sentence could be carried out at any minute, he sewed short sentences. The words on the left of the material were addressed to his wife (signed with the letter T.) and those on the right were for his son and daughter (signed, Papa).

This extraordinary message was passed to his daughter (his wife had already been deported to northern Kazakhstan) by one of Kozlovsky's cellmates, who, for reasons unknown, was released from prison. He smuggled the letter out by sewing it into the inside collar of his shirt.

In 1940, Kozlovsky's death sentence was unexpectedly transmuted to fifteen years' imprisonment. Before his departure, his daughter was permitted to see him. She said in her interview:

> My father came out all bandaged up and supported by two walking sticks. I was so horrified that I cried out, 'Papa, what has happened to you?' But he replied, 'Nothing. Everything is OK now, don't worry.' And straight away he began to ask how I was dressed. I had to lift up my foot and show him that I had galoshes and that my feet were dry. He was so happy to hear that I had earned a place at university, so very happy.

A month before the outbreak of war, Kozlovsky was transferred to Orlovsky Prison in the city of Oryol. Before he was moved, his daughter was permitted one final visit. It was to be the last time she saw her father.

BETTY,

ALL MY THOUGHTS AND
DREAMS ARE OF YOU
ALONE. T.

HOW I LOVED YOU – HOW
HARD IT IS TO HAVE LOST
YOU. T.

THERE IS NO NEED TO
CRY. I AM FOREVER WITH
YOU. T.

REMEMBER ME WITH
KIND WORDS. T.

NEVER DOUBT MY
FAITHFULNESS TO
THE PARTY, THE
MOTHERLAND AND YOU.
T.

NINA, ENYA!

I AM NOT YOUR ENEMY!

I FOUGHT IN 29 BATTLES,
IN THE BATTLE OF
WARSAW – FOR THE
MOTHERLAND, YOUR
HAPPINESS – I SHED
BLOOD TWICE. PAPA

CLOSER TO THE
KOMSOMOL AND PARTY! I
AM FOREVER WITH YOU.
PAPA

KEEP MY MEMORY SACRED.
I LOVED YOU MORE THAN LIFE.
LOOK AFTER YOUR MOTHER!
FAREWELL!

PAPA.
1. X. 39
KOZLOVSKY

He hugged me and lifted me onto his knee. Then he suddenly whispered in my ear, 'Nina, I am so afraid for you and Enechka. The war! War is starting, war is just around the corner!' I replied, 'What are you saying, Papa! We are on such friendly terms! We exchange kisses with Ribbentrop! What war?'

He replied, 'a pig cannot be a goose's friend.' War is coming, Nina. Be careful.'

Бетя?

К тебе одной все
мои думы и мечты.
                Т.

Как я любил тебя,
    как тяжело —
— потеряв тебя.
                Т.

Не надо слез.

Я вечно с тобой.

Добрым словом
        Т.

Меня вспоминай.
                Т.

Нина, Эня?

Я не враг вам?

Я был в 29 боях, в
битве под Варшавой, за
Родину — счастье ваше —

дважды пролил кровь.
                папа.

Ближе к комсомолу,
    к партии?

Я вечно с вами.
                папа.

Никогда не сомневайтесь в моей
честности перед партией, Родиной и Вами.
                            Т.

Свято храните обо мне память.

Любил вас — больше жизни.

Берегите маму?

Прощайте?

папа.
1. X. 39.
Козловский.

My father was an incredible person. I adored him. I loved him more than I loved my mother because he was unbelievably inquisitive. I remember an occasion before his arrest, when he fell ill. I must have been about fifteen at the time. I saw that he was lying down and reading a very thick book, so I went up to him and asked, 'Papa, what book is that?' And he replied, 'Differential equations.' Eyes on stalks, I asked, 'But why do you need to know about that?' And he said, 'You can't imagine how interesting it is.' My father also drew beautifully and had a fine understanding of art.

Anatoly Kozlovsky was not mistaken in predicting that war would soon be upon them. But he could not possibly have foreseen the fatal impact that the whirlwind of the German offensive would have upon his sentence. He was shot in the Medvedev Forest on the outskirts of Oryol on 11 September 1941 alongside many of his fellow inmates at the Orlovsky Prison. The mass shooting had been initiated by Lavrentiy Beria,* who on 6 September 1941 had sent Stalin a list with the names of 170 prisoners to whom he advocated meting out 'the highest measure of punishment'. The list is said to have included individuals who were alleged to have 'spread defeatism' among the prisoners and were attempting to escape, so as to begin their 'subversive activities' anew. Among the prisoners executed on that day were several prominent state and political figures, including Maria Spiridonova,† Olga Kameneva‡ and Christian Rakovsky.§

---

* Lavrentiy Beria was the infamous chief of the Soviet secret police under Stalin. He played a major role in the brutal mass purges of the 1930s.

† Maria Spiridonova was a Russian socialist revolutionary who spent eleven years in a Siberian prison before the Revolution for the assassination of a police officer. She was released in 1917, but arrested again in 1937 and sentenced to twenty-five years in the Gulag. However, following hunger strikes she was sent to Oryol Prison where she was held in isolation before being shot in 1941.

‡ Olga Kameneva was Leon Trotsky's younger sister. She was a Bolshevik revolutionary and Soviet politician and was arrested in 1936 following the arrest of her husband, Lev Kamenev (a leading Bolshevik and prominent Soviet politician).

§ Christian Rakovsky was a Soviet socialist revolutionary (of Bulgarian origin) and former member of Leon Trotsky's Left Opposition (he broke with Trotsky in 1934). In 1938 he was put on trial (along with Lev Kamenev), accused of conspiring to overthrow Stalin.

Anatoly Kozlovsky's son, Engels, volunteered for the front during the war. He fought in the Black Sea Fleet Marine Corps and died on 26 January 1944. His daughter, Nina, graduated from the Philology Department of Moscow State University. She taught Russian language and literature in schools in Cheboksary until her retirement.

Victor Mamaladze

'My dearest daddy . . .'

From the memoirs of Irma
Mamaladze.

It is one of my most painful memories.
I am in Tibilisi, [Georgia,] eight years
old and sitting at the dinner table,
chewing on the end of a wooden
pencil. A sheet of paper, torn from
an exercise book, lies in front of me,
on which are written the words, 'My
dearest daddy . . .'

Victor Mamaladze, early 1930s.

I cannot think what to write next –
I do not understand how and what I am supposed to write to a
stranger about whom I know only that he is my father and that
he is 'doing time'. The words 'doing time' are familiar. Most of
my aunts' husbands are in prison, as well as my aunts on both
my mother's and father's sides. My cousin is doing time, and
so are the husband and son of our neighbour with the huge
balcony, onto which the doors of our apartment open out. Life
is cramped and ordinary, and I am already aware that we should
consider ourselves 'lucky' because my father is only in prison,
whereas the husbands of two of my aunts have been shot. I
began to comprehend the horror of this word at the age of

three, through the tears in the eyes of my father's cousin Tamara who was living with us. Her husband, Herman Lomtatidze, had been shot in 1937 without a trial of any kind, and my aunt cried for him for a year. She cried for him, and for her wasted youth, and for her son, who was just five years older than me and had been left without a father.

My mother's anger frightened me. 'Why?' she would ask, 'why are you incapable of writing your father a decent letter when he loves you so much and so looks forward to them?'

I knew that he loved me, but today I recognise that this knowledge was purely cerebral; it did not affect me either way. What could I possibly write about? He didn't know any of my friends. My dreams of going to ballet school had been categorically quashed. The books that I was reading were too long to write about, and would he have heard of them anyway? Harried by my mother, I forced out a few meaningless words, too young to realise the bitterness, hurt and despair that they could sow.

I was two years old when my father saw us for the last time. He was a power engineer and as a very young man he had been involved in the launch of the Zemo-Avchala Hydroelectric Power Plant outside Tbilisi, which had been a hydroelectric giant of its day. He worked for a short time as the head engineer at GruzEnergo (Georgian Energy) from where he was

transferred to Moscow, with MosEnergo. My father was a talented engineer and I remember seeing pages of paper embossed with words that I did not understand, such as 'certificate of grant of patent'. During a later wave of terror and arrests, my mother destroyed these patents, along with all of my father's documents, for fear that she too might be subjected to scrutiny.

Irma Mamaladze, first year of school, Tbilisi, 1949.

My father's case file contains information affirming that when the war broke out, he was working as head of the Construction Department at the USSR People's Commissariat of Defence in Moscow. He was sent for further training at the Kuibyshev Military Engineering Academy in Moscow, which was later evacuated to Frunze*, but my mother and I did not go with him; instead he sent us to stay with his parents in Tbilisi. Before he left, my father managed to travel from Moscow to spend a couple of days with us in Tbilisi and during this final meeting he gave us one small passport-sized photograph of himself, dressed in his military uniform. It is most likely that it was on this trip that he encountered the distant relative and acquaintance who shortly afterwards denounced him to the authorities.

My father was arrested in Frunze in May 1942. I never saw the case materials – according to the Georgian Ministry of Internal Affairs, they were destroyed in a fire that broke out in the early 1990s in the building containing the KGB archives in Tbilisi.

Victor Mamaladze, Moscow, 1942.

He was taken from Frunze to Tbilisi, since it was there that he was accused of conducting underground activities (despite the fact that it had been more than ten years since he had lived in Georgia's capital). For almost a year, he was held in the basement cells of the NKVD headquarters in Tbilisi. Nobody had any idea where he had gone; my mother sent letters to everyone she thought could possibly know of his whereabouts, but they all went unanswered. She was quite literally out of her mind with worry. It was my grandfather who, quite by chance, found out what had happened when he bumped into an old school friend on the street one day. The friend quietly told him that his son,

* Today Bishkek, in Kyrgystan.

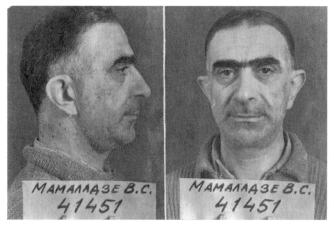

Prison photograph of Victor Mamaladze, Frunze, 1942.

who worked for the NKVD, had seen Victor there, and had described him as looking 'in a terrible way'.

My father was sentenced by the Special Board of NKVD, in accordance with Articles 58-10 and 58-11, to ten years in a corrective labour facility. He was sent to a camp near Aktyubinsk* in Kazakhstan, and so began his life as a convict, and our lives as associates of an enemy of the people. Our lives, as was the case for many others at that time, were testing, impoverished and uncertain. By the time the war ended, my mother was unable to return to her former apartment in Moscow – it was now a closed city, and anybody wishing to enter was required to obtain permission. She was also afraid of encountering my father's former acquaintances and co-workers. All that my mother latterly remembered of the ten short years that she had spent with my father was their cosy Moscow apartment, strolls with the nanny and pram around Devichye Polye and a single trip that she had taken with my father to a sanatorium for the People's Commissariat for Heavy Industry in Sochi.

Letters from my father arrived at regular, albeit extended, intervals. The days that we received them were always celebration days for my mother, and news that a letter had arrived would

---

* Today Aktobe.

Victor Mamaladze with
his wife, Tamara, Sochi,
1938.

spread like wildfire among our relatives. Within a day or two, the surviving aunts and every one of my father's cousins and second cousins would have come to visit. Each would read the letter to herself, before reading it aloud and voicing her thoughts. The tone of his letters was always upbeat and caring, and the aunts would invariably try to bring my mother some comfort. 'See,' they would say, 'he's fine. He is working hard and they will reduce his sentence. They will definitely reduce his sentence.'

They comforted her and cried together, and then they would begin to sing quietly in unison. This is how I was introduced to Georgian vocal harmonies.

I remember very little about those letters, but there is one that stands out in my memory. I wholeheartedly believed my father when he said that, come what may, he would return and we would all be together again. I was confident that he would do everything in his power to make this happen. He believed

that his sentence would be reduced if he worked hard, and only somebody truly heartless could dismiss this faith as naivety.

Fearing that she too was likely to be arrested, and afraid that the letters could be used as evidence against her, my mother destroyed almost all of them at the end of the 1940s. One of his later letters addressed to me survived, however, along with several drawings, which my mother cut out and kept for me from the postcards that my father sometimes enclosed. These notecards would invariably be decorated on one side with paintings of landscapes or wild animals, and my aunts would puzzle for hours over where he could possibly have managed to lay his hands on the paints. The answer became apparent many years later upon reading his case files.

It transpired that my father had been put to work in some sort of laboratory at the Aktyubinsk labour camp, having been transferred from the Ozerlag (a special camp for political prisoners) as a specialist engineer (intelligent engineers were sometimes valued by the Gulag authorities). It was most likely some kind of *sharashka*.* When construction work began on the foundations of the reservoir and roads for the planned Bratsk Hydroelectric Power Station (HEP), he was transferred

---

* Prison jargon for the secret scientific research and development laboratories that operated within the Soviet Gulag system. Living conditions for prisoners working in these institutions were often better than in the main camps, and rather than carrying out punishing manual labour, the scientists and engineers in *sharashkas* worked on solving scientific and technological problems for the state.

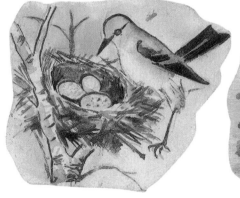

to the Angarlag, a labour camp near the village of Zayarsk in the Irkutsk region and not far from the city now known as Bratsk. My father was involved in the construction of a bridge across the Angara River and I remember him writing to tell my mother that he was now required to retrain himself from an HEP station engineer, to a bridge construction expert. He also sent us a clipping from the camp newspaper in which 'convict Mamaladze, acting Head of Construction' was praised for his work. The bridge was demolished when the reservoir was completed.

Bridge across the Angara River engineered by V. Mamaladze.

My father did not live to see out his sentence. He died aged forty-eight from a heart attack in the barracks one night, just six months before he was due to be released. We first heard the news in a letter from one of his friends at the camp, which was followed by an official notification from the camp authorities diagnosing him posthumously with 'stomach cancer'.

Many years later, I read a report by the camp doctor, which said that my father was diagnosed with 'acute heart failure' and a second document which stated that he had been buried 'in a coffin, in his underwear, with head facing east'. Tradition in this instance evidently proved stronger than the Gulag system. And yet all they could offer in recognition of years of gruelling labour was a separate grave, a coffin and a burial place that faced the sunrise.

Irma Mamaladze's heartbreaking memoirs require no further explanation, but Memorial would like to share a few further details extracted from her father's case files.

Victor Mamaladze was born in Tbilisi in 1902. He graduated from a university technical college in 1926 having specialised in technical engineering, and was employed to engineer the construction of Georgia's pioneering energy project, the Zemo-Avchala Hydroelectric Power Plant, alongside a number of other power plants in the south Caucasus. Having proven himself to be a talented engineer, he was put in charge of Mosenergo's high voltage power lines and became closely involved in the construction of the Stalinogorsk State Regional Power Station. He later became chief engineer and head of construction at both the Voronezh Power Plant and the Zakamsk Thermal Power Station. By the time war broke out, Mamaladze had been appointed chief engineer in the construction department of the USSR People's Commissariat of Defence. The country was preparing for war, so the young engineer was sent to further his knowledge at the Kuibyshev Military Engineering Academy. Mamaladze was married by this time and in 1940 his wife, Tamara, gave birth to their daughter, Irma. Two years later, he was promoted to major and appointed assistant divisional commander in the Central Asian Military District.

His good fortune ran out in June 1942, when he decided to break his journey to Frunze (to where the Kuibyshev Military Engineering Academy had been evacuated) at his parents' home in Tbilisi, where Tamara and Irma had been living since the outbreak of war. On the train, he struck up a conversation with a fellow passenger, who turned out to be a distant relation. The traveller informed upon him to the NKVD, claiming that Mamaladze had held an 'anti-Soviet conversation' with him and divulged information about an 'enemy' organisation operating in Tbilisi. Mamaladze was arrested in June 1942 and sent to Aktyubinsk to serve out his ten-year sentence.

Upon his arrival at the camp, Mamalazde wrote fifteen letters to the highest-ranking people he could think of, including Stalin and Beria, in an effort to prove his innocence to the authorities. As evidence of his dedication to the motherland, he cited letters that he had written to his wife prior to his arrest, 'where I promised to fight the enemy to victory's finale, or until I die', and in which he asked to be sent to the war 'into the front line of fire'.

Both during and after the war, it was Mamaladze's conscience, rather than a sense of fear, that motivated him in his work. So dedicated was he to his projects that even the management of the Aktyubinsk building trust (Aktyubstroy), for whom he worked during his years in the camp, petitioned on his behalf for his early release.

The following is an extract from a labour camp work reference for Victor Mamaladze:

> Prisoner Mamaladze, V. S. has shown himself to be an experienced engineer and worker. [. . .] He does a significant amount to improve technical operations at the building trust and works hard on plans for industrial and residential construction projects. Meanwhile, he also carries out substitution work, providing numerous viable alternatives to materials of which there is a deficit. In view of his conscientious approach to all the tasks set to him and the initiative that he has shown, he fully deserves to be considered for an early release.

The camp newspaper also commented upon Mamaladze's efficiency: 'Engineer Mamaladze has put forward a valuable and efficient suggestion on methods of preparing concrete using vacuum pressure. [. . .] This method can be successfully applied to any type of concrete structure or product . . .'

Sadly, all efforts to change the course of his fate proved

futile. The letters that he sent to high-ranking officials went unanswered and the petitions for his release were dismissed. In March 1949, three years before the end of his sentence, Mamaladze was transported to the Ozerlag and the following summer he was moved again, this time to the Angarlag, where he was to work as a specialist engineer.

Two final documents from November 1950 are tucked in Mamaladze's case file. The first is a notice of death, which reports that he died as a result of cardiac failure. The second is a note of burial.

All that remains of this remarkable man and the only mementos by which his daughter can remember him are a few family photographs and a handful of drawings cut from the letters that he sent home from the camps.

In her memoirs Irma Mamaladze wrote:

> With Memorial's help, I travelled to Irkutsk in the summer of 2010 to access my father's case and camp files, which had been preserved in the archives of the city's central branch of the Ministry of Internal Affairs. Only somebody who has been through the same ordeal could possibly understand how I felt as I sat at the table with my father's yellow file before me. Its contents accounted for almost nine years of his life in the camps. I am so thankful to Irkutsk's archivists and so grateful for their help, kindness and compassion.
>
> Afterwards, I went on to Zayarsk, but it must be said that this would have been impossible without the help of Memorial's employees: Alyona Kozlova, Sasha Mironov and Slava Kudashkin. I will always be hugely grateful for their efforts, as well as for the help of the rector of Bratsk University. I also have very fond memories of Sergei Kirillovich Plyushchenkov and the camp historian from Chuna – a former camp village – who showed me all that remains of the former camp cemeteries.

Almost nothing remains of Zayarsk, with the exception of a scattering of rickety houses whose purpose is unclear. The roads around the village are a sea of mud and the town cemetery is half-abandoned. A Russian flag flutters above a building that once served as a post office. The village is entirely cut off from civilisation. People say that planes used to fly to Zayarsk, but not even a trace of a runway remains. Spring floods and howling winds descend upon the taiga, carving out gullies in the landscape down which trees slide until they reach the water. There they remain, as if turned to stone. The boundless mirror of the Bratsk Sea has pulled a veil over camp, graves and dreams. It is a place of eternal calm.

You are here somewhere, my darling Papa. I came to find you. Forgive me.

Irma Mamaladze graduated from the Philology Faculty at Tbilisi State University and went on to gain a degree in journalism from the Lomonosov Moscow State University. She became a successful journalist and in addition to writing a regular column in the *Literaturnaya Gazette*, she became deputy editor of the Moscow-based newspaper *Obshaya Gazeta*.

Afterword

By the award-winning Russian novelist Ludmila Ulitskaya

'I have only one wish – to see you again, and then die.
I need nothing more.'

I too have a large folder at home that is filled with letters. A significant number of them were written from prisons and places of exile, but it was my grandfather, and not my father, who composed them. Above the table in my house hangs a photograph that I acquired recently from the KGB archives; it shows my grandfather photographed from the front, and in profile, and was taken immediately after his third arrest. His is the story of both our family and our country. It is the tale of our history . . .

Millions of the citizens of this great country were killed by the very utopia that they strived to create: that of a bright communist future. For decades, the country lived in an atmosphere of terror and heartache, fear and rapture, omnipresent denunciation and, particularly during the war years, patriotic hysteria. The dark side of this great project of communism was a system of countless labour camps in which those building this utopia were imprisoned in dreadful conditions, exhausted by hunger and back-breaking work. They were buried naked in unmarked graves, with identification labels on their feet. Millions of people were deprived of normal lives – a home, children, family and a career. Letters written home to wives and children provided those imprisoned with their sole connection to the outside world.

Most fathers never saw the children to whom they wrote again. Only a very few made it home – the majority were shot or perished in the camps, either from starvation or as a result of the punishing labour regimes. Many of the children to whom the letters were addressed are no longer alive, but Memorial's archives are safeguarding these precious epistles and testaments of great love.

This book provides first-hand testimony on the fate of sixteen men, using just some of the letters that somehow, miraculously, survived. For many years, even to keep such letters was an act of great bravery. The archives also contain numerous group photographs where the faces of the repressed have been cut or scribbled out with thick pen. The stories in this book constitute just a handful of the millions of similar lives that were torn apart and whose traces have been carried away and lost in the sweeping current of Russia's history. Theirs are the stories of innocent people who happened to fall into the meat-grinding machine of the Great Terror, and this makes the evidence that has survived even more precious. Who were these sixteen men whose letters form this collection? A former soldier, an accountant, a paediatrician, an engineer, an agriculturalist, a chemist, a botanist, an architect, an historian . . . They were all immensely cultured people; some were the nation's finest scientists and intellectual minds. Moreover, all were united not only by the love they shared for the children from whom they had been separated, but also by their overwhelming desire to play a part in their upbringing. They were determined to contribute to their mental development, guide their moral thinking and assist in their education.

The long and uninterrupted periods of incarceration and resultant separation served only to sharpen the fathers' acute feelings of love and heartache. Perhaps they would not have been such wonderful fathers and teachers had they remained at home with their families. Perhaps the humdrum of daily life would have distanced them from their children had their lives taken different courses. Either way, the ephemeral nature of the hope that these men harboured drove their relationships with their children to extraordinary heights. All sixteen fathers succeeded in accomplishing the remarkable feat of passing on to their children the advice they deemed most valuable. One appeals to his family 'never to doubt my allegiance to the Party, to the Motherland, or to you' while another reminds them that he 'voluntarily rejected all the advantages of the social class into which [he] was born'. Another writes of the 'detestable regime with which I have nothing in common [and] feel only vehement loathing'. This third man was the only one of the sixteen for whom the evidence used against him was not fabricated or falsified – he was a confirmed Trotskyist.

The men are united by a common tragedy, and their circumstances sharpened their feelings towards their children, magnifying and driving them to new heights. Their fatherly instincts compelled them to pass on to their children both their life skills, and the fundamentals of their professions, condensed down to their very limits in the letters. There is so much love, energy and concern bound within these now decrepit leaves of cheap paper, written in close, tiny hand so as to fit as much as possible onto a page. Indeed, to those imprisoned in the camps, even a page of paper, an envelope or a stamp was an exceptionally precious commodity.

While many of these letters were being written, another man, Daniil Andreev, was imprisoned in solitary confinement in Vladimir. The Russian mystic experienced a vision while in prison, as a consequence of which he devised a vast and complex religious and philosophical system, and presented a new world vision in a huge and mysterious treatise entitled *The Rose of the*

World. The novel is by no means a scientific breakthrough, but it does serve as an interesting reminder of a chapter in history, and it is undoubtedly the inspired feat of a creative soul. There is contained in this book, however, one simple idea conveyed in an unusually fresh and powerful way. The idea is this: in the universal battle between light and dark, love always prevails.

My Father's Letters is indelible proof that love conquers all.

Index of Places of Imprisonment

The following camps are just a small number of the individual units or small cooperatives of camps that together comprised the vast and complex Gulag system. Gulag was the acronym for the Chief Administration of Corrective Labour Camps. The names in brackets denote which of the individuals in this book were imprisoned in each particular camp.

Aktyubinlag: The Aktyubinsk Corrective Labour Camp and NKVD construction project site was established in 1940. The camp administration was in Aktyubinsk in the Kazakh Soviet Socialist Republic. Prisoners worked on the construction of the Aktyubinsk Ferroalloy Plant and were engaged in the mining and transport of chromite and nickeliferous iron ore, residential construction and the building of railways. The camp was closed in 1946. (Victor Mamaladze)

Angarlag: The Angarsk Corrective Labour Camp was established in 1947. From 1949 onwards, the camp administration was in Zayarsk. The prisoners laboured primarily on the construction of the Baikal–Amur railway line between Bratsk and Ust' Kut and the building of the bridge across the Angara River. The camp operated until 1960. (Victor Mamaladze)

Volgolag: The Volga Corrective Labour Camp was established in 1935 and incorporated a hydrological engineering unit. The camp administration was in Rybinsk. Prisoners worked on the NKVD's Volgastroy project, which included the construction of the Rybinsk, Uglich and Sheksna hydroelectric power plants. (Gavriil Gordon)

Dmitlag: The Dmitrovsky Corrective Labour Camp was established in 1932 and was the largest colony of OGPU-NKVD labour camps. It was purpose-built for the construction of the Moscow-Volga Canal, at the time named after Stalin, and its administrative headquarters were in Dmitrov. Prisoners also worked on the construction of the Northern Canal and the reconstruction of the Yauza River. The camp was closed in 1938. (Gavriil Gordon and Ivan Sukhanov)

Kargopollag: The Kargopol Corrective Labour Camp was established in 1937 and the administrative headquarters remained in Kargopol until 1940, when it moved to the Yertsevo railway station (on the northern railway line). Prisoners were primarily engaged in timber production. (Yevgeny Yablokov)

Karlag: The Karlag, or Karaganda Corrective Labour Camp, was one of the largest camps in the Gulag system. It was established in 1931 and the camp administration was in the small village of Dolinskoye in the Kazakh Soviet Socialist Republic. Prisoners worked in agriculture, industrial production, construction, coal mining and limestone quarrying. The camp closed in 1959. (Mikhail Bodrov, Friedrich Krause, Nikolai Lyubchenko)

Norillag: The Norilsk Corrective Labour Camp was established in 1935. Its primary focus was the construction of the Norilsk industrial region. Prisoners built the Norilsk Metallurgical Plant and mined copper-nickel ore and coal. They also built the Norilsk–Dudinka railway and many roads in the region. The camp was closed in 1956. (Victor Lunyov)

Special Camps: NKVD Special Camps, or Spetslag, was a system of labour camps with an especially strict regime. The system was established in 1948 for men and women accused of betraying the motherland, spying, terrorism and other political crimes of a 'particularly serious' nature. The prisoners were assigned to carry out heavy manual labour only. Their windows were barred, they were locked in their barracks at night and confined to them at all times when not working, and they wore numbers upon their clothes.

One such camp was the Ozerlag in the Irkutsk region, which comprised several camps between Bratsk and Tayshet. Prisoners worked on the construction of the Baikal–Amur railway line, timber production, the production of sawn timber, sleepers and material for the construction of wooden houses. The 'special camp' system was liquidated in 1954. (Victor Mamaladze)

Politisolator: Political isolation prison run by the GPU-OGPU that operated between 1920 and the early 1930s. They were used to imprison anybody that the authorities considered to be 'political'. This label was predominantly affixed to Socialist-Revolutionaries, Mensheviks, Anarchists and Socialist-Zionists. Later, it was expanded to encompass any member of an inner-party opposition movement. Political isolation prisons existed at Suzdal, Verkhneuralsk, Tobolsk, Chelyabinsk and Yaroslavl. (Mikhail Bodrov)

North-Eastern Corrective Labour Camp: This camp, also called the Sevvostlag, was established in 1932. It was the largest of Russia's Far Eastern camps, uniting all of the Kolyma corrective labour camps. The administrative centre of the Sevvostlag was in Magadan and the camp covered a vast territory that included today's Magadan area as well as parts of the Yakutia, Khabarovsk and Kamchatka regions. The work varied enormously but prisoners were mainly engaged in gold mining in the Kolyma and Indigirka river basins. A transportation point was built at the Sevvostlag between 1930 and 1940 for prisoners travelling to the furthest reaches of Kolyma and Vladivostok. (Mikhail Bodrov, Mikhail Lebedev, Mikhail Stroikov, Samuil Tieits)

Sevzheldorlag: Northern Railway Corrective Labour Camp established in 1938. The administrative office (*komendatura*) was in the village of Knyazh-Pogost in the Komi Autonomous Soviet Socialist Republic. Prisoners mainly worked on the construction of railways in the region and the camp was closed in 1950. (Boris Shustov)

Siblag: The Siberian Corrective Labour Camp was the largest in western Siberia, stretching across a territory comprising Omsk, Tomsk, Novosibirsk, the Kemerovo district and parts of the Altai and Krasnoyarsk regions. It was established in 1929 and the camp administration moved several times between Mariinsk and Novosibirsk. The prisoners worked in timber production, coal mining and the construction of roads and railways. The camp closed in the late 1960s. (Ivan Sukhanov, Vladimir Levitsky)

Siblag, Gorno-Shorskaya Komendatura: This administrative office was established in 1931, to manage 'special resettlers' passing through the Siblag from Western Siberia. More than 300,000 peasants, deported during the process of collectivisation, were concentrated in small villages (known as *spetsposyelki*), each with its own *komendatura*. Those managed by the Gorno-Shorskaya *komendatura* were put to work in timber production and in the building of the Gorno-Shorsky railway. (Vladimir Levitsky)

Solovki: The labour camp on Solovki was the OGPU's Solovki Special Purpose Camp. The first concentration camp was established on the Solovetsky Islands in 1923, and in 1930 all

OGPU concentration camps were renamed 'Corrective Labour Camps'. Prisoners on Solovki were mainly involved in timber production, peat harvesting and construction. The Solovki Special Purpose Camp was restructured in 1933 and became part of the White Sea–Baltic Corrective Labour Camp. A branch of the White Sea–Baltic camp remained on the island until 1937, when the Solovki Special Purpose Prison was established there by the Chief Directorate for State Security. (Alexei Vangenheim, Gavriil Gordon, Nikolai Lyubchenko)

Tagillag: The Nizhny Tagil Corrective Labour Camp operated from 1942 until 1953. The prisoners primarily worked in construction – they were responsible for building the numerous factories in the city of Nizhny Tagil. (Armin Stromberg)

Labour Army: Between 1942 and 1946, many members of the population were conscripted into compulsory 'work colonies' by their local *voenkomat* (see footnote on page 210). Having been disbanded in 1922, the Labour Army was re-established following Hitler's attack on Russia. A large portion of those conscripted into the Labour Army were Russian Germans, many of whom had already suffered during the deportation east of Russian ethnic Germans in 1941. The labour colonies were operated by the NKVD, and the conscripts were forced to carry out hard labour: coal mining, timber production and construction. As a rule, the living conditions of those in the Labour Army were very similar or identical to those of a labour camp prisoner. (Armin Stromberg)

Ukhtpechlag: The Ukhta-Pechorsk Corrective Labour Camp operated from 1931 until 1938. The camp administration was in the small village of Chibyu. Prisoners in this camp worked in the extraction of coal and oil as well as timber production and construction. (Ivan Sukhanov)

Index of Soviet Judicial Bodies

Military Collegium of the USSR Supreme Court
The highest organ of the Soviet military justicial system. When first established in 1924, it was designed to act as a supervisory body for military tribunals, approving their judicial decisions. In 1937–8 the Military Collegium of the USSR Supreme Court and its visiting sessions acted as a court of first instance, and delivered verdicts on what came to be known as 'Stalin's shooting lists' – the lists of individuals sentenced to death approved in advance by Stalin and his close associates. 'In accordance with legislation dated 1 December 1934', approximately 40,000 sentences were delivered (without witness statements, without challenges from any side and without the right to appeal). In the vast majority of these rulings, the defendants were sentenced to death. The Military Collegium of the USSR Supreme Court was responsible for cases relating to the more serious crimes – notably, betrayal of the motherland, espionage, terrorism and sabotage.

Collegium of the OGPU
A collective governing body presided over by the chairman of the OGPU. It succeeded the Collegium of the Cheka and the Collegium of the GPU (predecessors of the OGPU). The Council of People's Commissars of the Soviet Union approved all members of the Collegium of the OGPU. Aside from dealing with any issues specific to their department, the collegium

reserved the right to preside over any administrative or criminal cases of its choosing. The OGPU would then carry out the sentence, which might include a long term of incarceration or capital punishment. In cases ruled upon by the Collegium of the OGPU, defendants were denied the opportunity to defend themselves, and neither statements from witnesses, the prosecution, nor the defence were heard. This collegium was terminated in 1934, upon the formation of the NKVD (USSR).

Special Board of NKVD (OSO)
From 1924: Special Board of OGPU
From 1934: Special Board of the People's Commissariat of Internal Affairs
From 1946–53: Special Board of MGB USSR
From 1953: Special Board of MVD USSR
This was a special-purpose commission comprising the most senior figures in the security organs together with a representative from the public prosecutor's office. It was created to allow cases that fell within the OGPU's (NKVD-MVD-MGB) remit to be handled extrajudicially, and thus enabled the Special Board to deliver sentences on cases without considering statements from the defendant or witnesses, and without challenges from any side. Initially, the OSO had the authority to deport, exile or incarcerate a person in a political isolation camp or concentration camp for up to three years. A little later, in 1934, the maximum term was increased to five years. In April 1937, it was again increased, this time to eight years, and by September 1937 the maximum sentence had been extended to ten years. During the war years (1941–5), its powers were extended yet further, and the OSO was granted permission to sentence people to death. After the war, the maximum incarceration sentence was doubled to twenty (sometimes twenty-five) years. Those convicted could be sentenced to hard labour in a penal colony or a special camp for political prisoners, or exiled for an interminable length of

time. A ruling by the OSO was considered to be irreversible – a sentence could only be reconsidered by the OSO itself, not by the other judicial bodies. The Special Board of NKVD/MVD was dissolved on 1 September 1953.

Troika of NKVD

From 1937–8 this was an additional judicial body that drew from all of the different levels of regional NKVD directors (state, region, district). It was established to deliver sentences in the most widespread operation of repression in Soviet history – the so-called 'kulak operation', in accordance with order No 00447 of the USSR NKVD. The chairman of the troika was the director of the corresponding regional NKVD branch, and the regional Communist Party secretary (or other party representative) and public prosecutor filled the remaining two places. Sometimes the prosecutor was a senior member of the corresponding territorial executive branch of government. Cases were considered in the defendant's absence, so there was no right of appeal, and neither witness statements, nor challenges from any side were heard. In the space of a year the troikas passed sentences on approximately 800,000 people; over half were sentenced to death. Regional troikas also examined the cases of Gulag prisoners and those incarcerated in prisons run by the Chief Directorate for State Security. A case in point was the Troika of NKVD for the Leningrad region, which played a particularly significant role in sentencing those incarcerated within Solovki prison. This troika sentenced 1,825 people to death. Similarly, a troika for Dalstroy was created at Magadan for the purpose of sentencing those imprisoned within the Sevvostlag camp. It sentenced 7,000 Kolyma prisoners to death.

Chronology of Soviet Secret Police Agencies

1917–22 – Cheka
Abbreviation of VChK, an acronym for the All-Russian Extraordinary Commission Combating Counter-Revolution and Sabotage.

1922–3 – GPU
Acronym for State Political Directorate, operated by the NKVD (People's Commissariat for Internal Affairs). This reorganisation may have been an effort by the Bolshevik Politburo to bring the activities of the state security organs under their control. However, the organs prized their independence and, in under a year, they had succeeded in freeing themselves from subordination to the NKVD.

1923–34 – OGPU USSR
Acronym for Joint State Political Directive of the USSR. The OGPU was not under the subordination of the NKVD. Attached to the OGPU was the Special Board, which rendered extrajudicial decisions on sentences to labour camps, or the shooting of individuals convicted of certain crimes.

1934
The NKVD of the Russian Soviet Federative Socialist Republic becomes the all-union NKVD of the USSR.

1934–41 – NKVD USSR

The NKVD of the USSR incorporates the OGPU, which becomes the GUGB (Main Directorate for State Security). The GUGB was briefly separated out into the GUGB NKVD between 1941 and 1943, before being merged back in.

1943–6 – NKGB USSR

The NKVD was renamed NKGB (People's Commissariat of State Security).

1946–53 – MGB USSR

The NKGB was renamed MGB (Ministry of State Security).

1953–4 – MVD

Lavrentiy Beria merges the MGB into the MVD (Ministry of Internal Affairs).

1954–91 – KGB

Following Beria's execution, the secret police were once again separated from the Ministry of Internal Affairs and a newly independent force was created; the KGB (Committee of State Security).

Since the collapse of the Soviet Union in 1991, the KGB has ceased to function as a single entity. The responsibility of state security is now shared between several separate agencies including the SVR (Foreign Intelligence Service), the GRU (Main Directorate of the General Staff of the Armed Forces of the Russian Federation) and the FSB (Federal Security Service). The latter is the principal security agency operating in Russia today.

List of Abbreviations

Arkhbumstroy	Arkhangelsk Pulp and Paper Mill
CPO	Central Physics Observatory
Dalstroy	Far North Construction Trust
Glavnauk	General Directorate of Scientific, Museum and Scientific-Art Institutions of the People's Commissariat of the RSFSR
Gubprodkom	Provincial Food Committee
Gulag	General Directorate of Forced Labour Camps and Colonies of the NKVD (MVD) of the USSR
GULZHDS	Main Camp Directorate for Railway Construction of the NKVD (MVD)
Komsomol	All-Union Leninist Young Communist League
Narcomles	People's Commissariat of the Timber Industry
Narcompros	People's Commissariat of Education
Narkomzdrav	People's Commissariat of Public Health
Osoaviakhim	Society for the Defence, Aviation and Chemical Construction of the USSR
Sevvostlag	North-Eastern Corrective Labour Camp system
Sevzheldorlag	Northern Railway Corrective Labour Camp
SVITlag	NKVD North-Eastern Labour Camps
TSIK	Central Executive Committee

USVITlag	Directorate of the NKVD North-Eastern Corrective Labour Camps
Vkhutemas	Higher education training workshops for art and technical studies
VTSIK	All-Russian Central Executive Committee of the RSFSR
MID	USSR Ministry of Internal Affairs
Raizdrav	The Regional Public Health Care Administration
Sovnarkom	Council of People's Commissars

Acknowledgements

The 'MEMORIAL' International Historical, Educational, Human Rights and Charitable Society (Мемориа́л) publishing programme.

Editorial team: Alexander Daniel, Larisa Eremina, Elena Zhemkova, Tatyana Kasatkina, Nikita Okhotin, Yan Rachinsky, Arseny Roginsky (Chairman).

Edited by: Alena Kozlova, Nikolai Mikhailov, Irina Ostrovskaya and Svetlana Fadeeva.

Elena Zhemkova, Nikita Lomakin, Arseny Roginsky and Irina Sherbakova contributed to work on this volume.

For help in working on the book and the exhibition 'My Father's Letters', the editors would like to thank Valentin Grinchuk, Galina of Jordan, Vsevolod Luhovitsky, Peter Pasternak, Julia Reifshneider, Marina Rodionova, Ksenia Romanenko, Ilya Saratovsky, Pauline Guern, Ulyana Lukyanchenko and Nina Zuckerman.

Special thanks to the director of Agey Tomesh/WAM publishing company, Natalya Korneeva.

Thanks to the Heinrich Böll Foundation, Dmitry Zimin, the

Dynasty Institute and the Open Society for their ongoing support of the 'MEMORIAL' International Historical, Educational, Human Rights and Charitable Society (Мемориа́л).

The book was put together as part of the project 'The fates of the victims of political repression and the right to rehabilitation and memory'. To implement the project state support funds were granted in accordance with the Order of the President of the Russian Federation, 29 March 2013 No. 115-rp.

Memorial: Retaining Our Memory of History

Memorial is an international historical and educational charity, set up in 1988 on a groundswell of public opinion from different generations. Its supporters had very varied biographies, and sometimes divergent political outlooks. They were not only former political prisoners and their families, but young people and others in favour of establishing a democratic state under the rule of law.

Memorial's first chairman was Academician Andrey Sakharov. Today, Memorial is a network of dozens of organisations in Russia, Germany, Italy, France, the Czech Republic and Ukraine who conduct research and educational work and defend human rights. In 1991, on Memorial's initiative and with the society's participation, a law was passed on rehabilitation of victims of political repression. It declared 30 October a Day of Remembrance of Victims of Political Repression.

From the outset, Memorial has considered one of its principal tasks to be the creation of a tradition of informed remembrance of political repression in the USSR. An essential part of this work has been collecting and preserving the testimony of over 12 million people persecuted during the Stalin era. In the course of thirty years, Memorial has established the only systematic public archive of its kind in Russia: museum holdings, collections of documents, and a specialised library.

Another aspect of the work is restoring and making publicly available the identities and biographies of victims. A Book of Remembrance provides the foundation for an electronic database of more than 3 million victims of political repression.

Memorial organises discussions directly related to remembrance and analysis of current policy towards history.

The charity is constantly studying not only the means of transmitting historical memory from generation to generation, but actively encouraging this by organising a nationwide history essay competition for older school students on the topic of 'Man in History: Russia in the Twentieth Century'.

Memorial sees scholarly and research work as an integral part of its mission. Among its main projects are:

> – creating maps of the Gulag and a definitive work describing the Gulag system;
> – creating reference works giving the biographies of the organisers and perpetrators of the Terror;
> – studying the role and significance of social-democratic opposition to the Stalin regime;
> – researching the administrative structure and statistics of the Terror;
> – studying sites associated with the topography of the Terror;
> – studying family memories of the Terror;
> – monitoring museum collections relevant to the history of the Gulag;
> – studying the fate of different national and religious groups of victims of political repression.

Memorial's archival and museum collections

Memorial's archive began acquiring materials from the very inception of the society in 1989, when victims of repression, their relatives and friends began passing documents, photographs and manuscript memoirs from their family archives to the movement's activists. The archive consists of several themed collections.

Archive of the History of Political Repression in the USSR, 1917–56

The backbone of this collection is personal files of people who were persecuted: shot, sentenced to prison camp terms, exiled, or 'dekulakised' in the case of more prosperous peasants. The collection contains in excess of 60,000 personal archives. These consist of such materials directly related to the persecution as originals and copies of official arrest warrants, records of searches; pages from archival, criminal, prison camp or surveillance files; notifications of sentence, death certificates, certificates of release and rehabilitation; and such personal documents as lists of parcels sent to prisons and camps, and appeals by prisoners and relatives for a review of their case. There are also documents from the period of detention: character references, poetry, posters for camp amateur performances, certificates of good behaviour, home-made cards, sheet music, and personal notes.

Correspondence between prisoners and their families is of particular interest. This includes not only officially authorised correspondence, read and often with deletions by the censor, but also letters passed to the outside world illegally: snatches of news from prison trains in transit, notes scrawled on fabric or cigarette paper and hidden in the seams of clothing or in buttons. The personal files also contain documents from before arrest: birth certificates, school-leaving and degree certificates, membership cards of various organisations, service records, diplomas and award certificates, letters, family and work photographs, and the like.

Memoir and Literary Works Collection

The Memoir and Literary Works Collection contains some 600 files and represents a unique source of personal testimony about life in the USSR in the twentieth century, about arrests, investigations, camps, and exiles (the latter reflecting the entire history and geography of the Gulag). In addition to memoirs, the archive includes collections of letters, diaries, sketches and articles, and literary and journalistic works. Most of these texts have never been published.

Archive of the 'Victims of Two Dictatorships' Programme

This archive of materials, on the fate of Soviet people deported to perform forced labour in Germany during World War II, contains some 400,000 case files. Many of these people were subjected to harassment and persecution when they returned to the USSR. The files contain biographical information, letters and memoirs, documents issued by the German administration; documentation of their passage through "filtration" when they were repatriated; data from Soviet state and ministry archives, as well as from the International Tracing Service of the Red Cross; personal papers (photographs, letters and postcards from Germany and filtration camps).

A database on individuals has been compiled, drawing on the archive's holdings, which, among other things, gives information on where "Ostarbeiter", slave labourers from the East, lived and worked in Nazi Germany.

Archive of the History of Dissidence in the USSR, 1953–87

Memorial's collection of documents on the history of dissidence in the post-Stalin era is the largest in Russia and one of the most extensive in the world. It comprises 125 holdings and collections, as well as archive of photos and collection of rare publications which appeared in very limited editions.

The holding comprises some 400,000 sheets. These include a collection of Samizdat works assembled by Memorial International. Personal collections and archives include letters, diaries, memoirs, drafts of articles, and other working materials of prominent dissidents, totalling about 100 personal files. The archive contains photocopies of around 13,000 index cards of prisoners sentenced in the 1950s to 1980s for political and dissident activities. The collection is an important source for research into oppositional social and political activity and the repressive policies of the USSR during this period. Samizdat and other materials connected with dissidence come in a variety of shapes and forms: typescripts, photocopies, home-made albums with illustrations. Some are truly unique: a letter from exile typed on cloth, a tape recording made secretly in the camp, and so on. The collection also contains some 5,000 photographs.

The Centre for Oral History and Biography
The Centre has ongoing projects on Women's Memories of the Gulag and Children of 'Algeria' [the Akmolinsk Camp for Wives of Traitors to the Fatherland, opened in January 1938], which have recordings of some 300 interviews, as well as thousands of documents, photographs, memoirs, letters and diaries, depicting the fate of wives of 'traitors to the fatherland', who were sent off to the camps, and of their children, who were placed in 'orphanages'. The collected materials and, in particular, the oral evidence, enable us to trace how the history of mothers despatched to the Gulag affected the biography and destiny of their children, and to re-assess the traumatic experience of families under the Soviet system.

In the course of the projects Survivors of Mauthausen, and Forced Labour in National Socialist Germany, about 300 audio and video interviews were recorded with former prisoners of concentration camps and Ostarbeiter, which portray the tragic vicissitudes of these people during the war and their long experience of discrimination in the post-war era.

Memorial Museum Collection

The Memorial Museum Collection began to be formed as early as 1988. Along with documents, relatives of the persecuted brought memorabilia, drawings and photographs for safekeeping by Memorial, and in 1990 a museum was set up. The main source of acquisitions was families of the persecuted, which had kept relics, paintings and drawings; some of the exhibits were acquired on expeditions to the sites of former camps. The museum currently houses some 6,000 items. With 1,500 exhibits, this is the world's largest collection of works created in captivity. The greater part of the collection is paintings and drawings by imprisoned artists: genre drawings, portraits, interiors, landscapes, and sketches for scenery and costumes for productions in the camp theatres. Some of them are by famous artists who ended up in the camps and exile.

Closely related to the museum collection are some 12,000 works in the photograph archive. These are originals or copies of documentary photographs depicting the history of political repression in the USSR from the 1920s to the 1980s, the life and labour of the prisoners of the Gulag, the everyday life of the USSR, and Soviet propaganda.

ADDRESS:

Memorial International
5/10 Karetny Ryad,
Moscow 127006
Russia
tel. (+7 495) 650 7883
e-mail: nipc@memo.ru
websites: www.memo.ru;
           www.urokiistorii.ru